I0018737

Assembly Programming for Network

Development of Communication Protocols

Louis Madson

1

3

Discover other books in the Series

**"Assembly Programming for Beginners: Master
the Low Level and Control Hardware from
Scratch"**

**"Assembly Programming for Cyber
Security:Unleash the Power of Low-Level Code to
Break and Defend Systems"**

**"Assembly Programming for Computer
Architecture: Understanding the Hardware"**

**"Assembly Programming for Malware Analysis:
Malicious Software Development and Malware
Analysis with Assembly"**

**"Assembly Programming for Operating Systems:
Build Your Own OS from Scratch"**

Copyright © 2025 by Louis Madson.

All rights reserved. No part of this book may be used or reproduced in any form whatsoever without written permission except in the case of brief quotations in critical articles or reviews.

Printed in the United States of America.

For more information, or to book an event, contact :
(Email & Website)

Book design by Louis Madson
Cover design by Louis Madson

Disclaimer

The information provided in *"Assembly Programming for Network: Development of Communication Protocols"* by Louis Madson is for educational and informational purposes only.

This Book is designed to introduce readers to the fundamentals of assembly programming and low-level hardware control. The author and publisher make no representations or warranties regarding the accuracy, completeness, or applicability of the content.

Introduction

In a world that is becoming increasingly interconnected, the foundation of effective communication is established by the protocols that dictate the transmission and reception of data across various networks. As devices interact with one another, it is crucial for developers, engineers, and technology enthusiasts to comprehend these protocols. This book, titled "Assembly Programming for Networks: Development of Communication Protocols," aims to clarify the complexities associated with network programming and equip you with a robust understanding of both assembly language and the development of communication protocols.

Assembly language, often considered a low-level programming language, provides unmatched control over hardware and system resources. By mastering assembly programming, you will gain a deeper understanding of the fundamental operations of computer systems, which will enable you to create optimized, high-performance applications. While higher-level programming languages tend to obscure many details of hardware interaction, assembly programming offers a distinctive viewpoint that is essential for effective protocol development.

In this book, we will explore the key concepts of networking and examine the nuances of protocol design. You will learn to leverage the capabilities of assembly programming to create resilient communication protocols, ensuring efficient data transfer and reliability within networks. Whether you are developing a straightforward device-to-device communication system or crafting a sophisticated protocol for large-scale applications, the skills you acquire in this text will be relevant across a diverse array of scenarios.

We will begin by establishing a strong foundation in networking principles, discussing key concepts such as TCP/IP stack architecture, data encapsulation, and error handling. With this knowledge, we will progressively transition into the assembly programming environment, exploring how to leverage low-level coding to implement networking protocols from the ground up.

Throughout the pages of this book, you will encounter practical examples, step-by-step tutorials, and hands- on projects that will reinforce your learning and empower you to apply your skills in real-world situations.

By the end of our journey, you will not only have a comprehensive understanding of assembly programming within the context of communication protocols, but you will also be equipped with the tools required to innovate and contribute to the ever-evolving landscape of network technology.

Whether you are a seasoned programmer looking to broaden your skill set or a newcomer eager to explore the intricacies of networking and assembly language, "Assembly Programming for Networks: Development of Communication Protocols" serves as your guide through this fascinating and vital intersection of technology. So, let us embark on this journey together and unravel the potential that lies in the union of assembly programming and networking protocols.

Chapter 1: Introduction to Assembly for Network Programming

As a cornerstone of contemporary software development, a solid grasp of networking principles can greatly augment a programmer's expertise. Although high-level programming languages predominantly shape the realm of network development, there exists a potent yet frequently neglected resource—assembly language. This chapter aims to connect the realms of low-level programming and networking, advocating for the inclusion of assembly language as an essential component of a network programmer's skill set.

1.1 The Importance of Assembly Language

Assembly language acts as a vital link between high-level programming languages and machine code, which is executed directly by a computer's CPU. Utilizing assembly language can provide numerous benefits in network programming, including enhanced performance, precise management of system resources, and a deeper comprehension of network operations at the hardware level.

While high-level languages such as Python, Java, and C# equip developers with the means to rapidly create intricate applications, they often obscure many critical details that are essential in scenarios where performance is crucial, such as real-time communication or environments with limited resources. For example, a thorough understanding of how data packets are formed, transmitted, and processed can significantly improve debugging methods and optimization techniques in the development of network applications.

1.2 The Role of Assembly Language in Networking

Networking fundamentally relies on the exchange of data between endpoints in a network. This exchange involves various protocols, such as HTTP, TCP/IP, and UDP. An understanding of these protocols at a low level can help developers create more efficient applications—something achievable through assembly programming.

Some specific areas where assembly can play a pivotal role include:

Packet Manipulation: At the heart of network programming lies packet manipulation. Using assembly language can enable developers to craft and parse packets with extreme efficiency. This is especially important in scenarios like network security, where understanding and modifying packets on the fly can lead to more robust defenses against attacks.

Performance Optimization: In high-stakes environments such as gaming, finance, or real-time communication, the speed of data processing can be crucial. By writing performance-critical code in assembly language, developers can minimize latency and improve throughput, thereby enhancing the overall user experience.

Direct Hardware Interaction: When dealing with embedded systems or specialized networking hardware, developers may require direct access to hardware controls that are not exposed by higher-level languages. Assembly provides the necessary constructs for this level of interaction, allowing programmers to create highly optimized and responsive network applications.

1.3 The Learning Journey

Despite its advantages, the barrier to entry for assembly language can be steep. With a syntax that differs significantly from high-level languages and a requirement for a solid understanding of computer architecture, many developers may shy away from it. However, a methodical approach can ease this learning curve.

In the subsequent chapters, we will explore:

The basic structure and syntax of assembly language.

How assembly interacts with the underlying hardware.

The intricacies of network protocols and how they can be implemented in assembly.

Case studies focusing on real-world applications developed in assembly language within networking contexts.

By the end of this book, readers will have a comprehensive understanding of how to effectively use assembly language for network programming, empowering them to tackle complex network problems and master the art of packet manipulation and data exchange.

While high-level programming languages dominate the field of network programming, the relevance of assembly language should not be underestimated. With its precision and performance capabilities, assembly can profoundly impact the development of efficient networking applications.

Understanding Low-Level Network Programming

This chapter will delve into the fundamentals of network protocols, socket programming, data transmission, and the intricacies of managing connections. By the end, you should have a solid grasp of low-level networking concepts and be prepared to implement your own network applications.

1. What is Low-Level Network Programming?

Low-level network programming refers to the programming techniques used to directly interact with the hardware and software resources of a network. Unlike high-level abstractions provided by frameworks or libraries, low-level programming leans on lower layers of the OSI (Open Systems Interconnection) model, mainly focusing on the Transport Layer (Layer 4) and Application Layer (Layer 7). This type of programming grants developers granular control over data transmission, error handling, and connection management.

1.1 Importance of Low-Level Networking

Efficiency: Low-level programming allows for optimization, reducing overhead and ensuring that applications run as quickly and as efficiently as possible.

Control: Developers have precise control over network functionalities such as packet creation, encoding, and error detection, allowing them to handle specific use cases more effectively.

Customization: Tailor networking protocols and

features to meet unique application requirements, enabling enhanced performance and support for bespoke use cases.

Debugging: It can enhance debugging capabilities by providing insights into the data being sent and received, as developers can monitor and manipulate lower-level communications.

2. Network Protocols

Understanding network protocols is foundational to low-level networking. A protocol is a set of rules governing how data is transmitted over a network. Here, we'll discuss key protocols relevant to low-level network programming.

2.1 Transmission Control Protocol (TCP)

TCP is a connection-oriented protocol that ensures reliable data transmission. It establishes a connection before transmitting data, verifies that packets arrive correctly, and allows for error detection and recovery. Essential features of TCP include:

Connection Management: Establishment through a three-way handshake (SYN, SYN-ACK, ACK).

Data Segmentation: Divides large messages into smaller packets.

Flow Control: Manages sender and receiver's data rates to prevent packet loss. ### 2.2 User Datagram Protocol (UDP)

In contrast to TCP, UDP is a connectionless protocol, which means it does not guarantee delivery, ordering,

or error recovery. It is faster and requires less overhead, making it appropriate for real-time applications such as gaming or voice over IP (VoIP). Key characteristics include:

Simplicity: Fewer features mean reduced complexity and faster performance.

No Guarantees: It does not provide reliability, so lost packets are not retransmitted. ### 2.3 Internet Protocol (IP)

IP is responsible for routing packets of data across a network. It determines how packets are addressed and sent to their destination. Versions include IPv4 and IPv6, with IPv6 being important for future-proofing applications due to its expanded address space.

3. Sockets: The Foundation of Network Communication

A socket is an endpoint for sending or receiving data across a network. Low-level network programming often involves working with sockets to create, send, and receive messages over the network.

3.1 Creating Sockets

In most programming languages, creating a socket usually involves specifying the protocol (TCP/UDP) and binding it to an IP address and port number. Here's a simple example in Python for creating a TCP socket:

```python
```python import socket

# Creating a TCP socket

server_socket    =    socket.socket(socket.AF_INET, socket.SOCK_STREAM)

# Binding the socket to an IP address and port
```
```

```
server_socket.bind(('localhost', 8080))
```

```
# Listening for incoming connections
server_socket.listen(5)
```
```

### 3.2 Connecting Sockets

For client-side applications, the process includes identifying the server through the IP address and port before establishing a connection. Here's how you can connect a client socket to a server:

```python
client_socket = socket.socket(socket.AF_INET, socket.SOCK_STREAM)
client_socket.connect(('localhost', 8080))
```
```

3.3 Sending and Receiving Data

Once a connection is established, data can be sent and received through the socket:

```python
# Sending data client_socket.sendall(b'Hello, Server!')
```

```
# Receiving data
```

```
data = client_socket.recv(1024) print('Received', repr(data))
```
```

### 3.4 Closing Sockets

It's crucial to properly close sockets to free up resources and avoid memory leaks. This can be done using:

15
```

```python
client_socket.close()
server_socket.close()
```

4. Error Handling in Network Programming

Network applications must cope with unpredictable network conditions. Therefore, robust error handling is paramount. Errors may arise from connection interruptions, packet loss, or timeouts. Here are some strategies:

Timeouts: Set socket timeouts to avoid waiting indefinitely.

Retries: Implement resend mechanisms for lost packets, especially in TCP connections.

Exception Handling: Use try-except blocks to gracefully handle exceptions and provide meaningful error messages.

By understanding protocols, sockets, and implementing robust error handling, you can create applications that are not only efficient but also resilient to network failures.

Setting Up an Assembly Development Environment for Networking

This chapter is dedicated to guiding you through setting up a development environment tailored for assembly language programming with a focus on networking. By the end of this chapter, you will be equipped with the necessary tools, configurations, and knowledge to start building your own network applications in assembly.

1. Understanding Assembly Language

Before diving into the setup, it's crucial to understand what assembly language is and why it matters in networking. Assembly language is a low-level programming language that is closely related to machine code and architecture-specific instructions. It allows developers to write highly efficient code with control over hardware and memory management. In networking, where performance is critical, assembly programming can yield significant benefits.

1.1 Why Assembly for Networking?

Performance: Assembly allows for optimization that high-level languages cannot achieve.

Hardware Access: Direct manipulation of hardware resources can lead to more efficient network operations.

Protocol Implementation: Writing custom protocols requires deep understanding and fine control—both of which assembly provides.

2. Prerequisites

Before setting up your assembly development environment, ensure you have the following prerequisites:

Basic Knowledge of Networking: Understand TCP/IP, UDP, and how networking stacks operate.

Familiarity with Assembly Language: While not mandatory, having a foundational understanding can help you grasp advanced concepts better.

Hardware: A computer with a compatible operating

system (Windows, Linux, or macOS). ## 3. Tools Required for Assembly Development

3.1 Assembler

An assembler is a crucial tool for converting assembly language into machine code. Choose an assembler based on your operating system:

NASM (Netwide Assembler): A popular cross-platform assembler that supports Intel syntax.

MASM (Microsoft Macro Assembler): For Windows environments, optimizing for x86 architecture.

FASM (Flat Assembler): Known for its speed and simplicity, also cross-platform. ### 3.2 Debugger

Debugging is an essential part of development. A good debugger will allow you to step through your code, inspect memory, and set breakpoints. Options include:

GDB (GNU Debugger): A powerful debugger for Linux and macOS users.

WinDbg: A sophisticated debugger for Windows applications.

3.3 Integrated Development Environment (IDE)

While assembly programming can be done with simple text editors, using an IDE can streamline development. Consider:

Visual Studio Code: Supports assembly with various extensions for syntax highlighting and debugging.

Eclipse with the CDT plugin: Suitable for more

extensive projects. ## 4. Setting Up Your Environment ### 4.1 Installation Steps #### On Linux:

Install NASM:

```bash
sudo apt update
sudo apt install nasm
```

Install GDB:

```bash
sudo apt install gdb
```

Install Visual Studio Code or any preferred IDE:

Follow the official installation guide from the [VS Code website](https://code.visualstudio.com/docs/setup/setup-overview).

On Windows:

Download and Install NASM:

Download the Windows installer from the [NASM website](https://www.nasm.us/) and follow the installation instructions.

Install WinDbg:

Get WinDbg through the Windows SDK or install it via the Microsoft Store.

Set up Visual Studio Community Edition:

Download from the [Visual Studio

website](https://visualstudio.microsoft.com/) and follow the prompts. ### 4.2 Network Libraries and Tools

In addition to the assembler and debugger, ensure you have the necessary networking libraries:

Winsock (Windows): This API allows for network programming, providing functions for socket-based communications.

Berkeley Sockets (Linux/macOS): The standard API for socket programming in Unix-like systems. ### 4.3 Environment Variables

After installation, set environment variables to make the tools accessible from the command line.

For example, on Linux, you can add to the `.bashrc` or `.bash_profile`:

```bash
export PATH=$PATH:/path/to/nasm
```

5. First Steps in Assembly Networking

With your environment set up, it's time to write and run a basic network program. Let's create a simple TCP server in NASM for Linux.

```asm
section .data
port db '8080'
; Additional data for socket programming
section .text global _start
```

```
_start:

; Load socket programming system calls

; Create a socket, bind to the address, listen, accept
connections

; Exit cleanly

mov rax, 60          ; syscall: exit xor rdi, rdi    ; status: 0
syscall
```

Compile and run your code:

```bash
nasm -f elf64 server.asm -o server.o ld server.o -o server -
no-pie

./server
```

6. Troubleshooting Common Issues

Linking Errors: Ensure that you've linked with the appropriate networking libraries.

Permission Issues: Running servers often requires elevated privileges; consider using `sudo` for port numbers below 1024.

Networking Permissions: Ensure your firewall or network settings allow for the application's traffic.

Setting up your assembly development environment for networking is an essential first step in leveraging the benefits of low-level programming. With the tools and steps discussed in this chapter, you should be equipped to begin developing efficient and powerful network applications using assembly language.

Chapter 2: Fundamentals of Network Communication

In an increasingly interconnected world, understanding the fundamentals of network communication is essential. This chapter delves into the core concepts that form the foundation of how data is transmitted, received, and understood across various network types. By grasping these principles, one can develop a greater appreciation for the intricacies of modern communication systems.

2.1 What is Network Communication?

Network communication refers to the exchange of data between devices or systems over a network. This can involve a variety of hardware, software, and protocols that work together to ensure data is transmitted efficiently and accurately. The underlying goal is to facilitate effective communication between devices, which can range from computers and servers to mobile phones and IoT devices.

2.2 The Basic Components of Network Communication

To understand how network communication functions, it is essential to identify its primary components: ### 2.2.1 Devices

Devices, also known as hosts, are endpoints in a network that send and receive data. Common examples include computers, smartphones, servers, and network printers. Each device typically has a unique identifier known as an IP address, which allows it to be recognized on the network.

2.2.2 Medium

The medium refers to the physical or logical pathways

through which data travels. This can include wired connections, such as Ethernet cables, as well as wireless connections, like Wi-Fi or cellular signals. The choice of medium impacts the speed, reliability, and range of communication.

2.2.3 Protocols

Protocols are standardized rules and conventions that govern how data is transmitted and received over a network. They ensure that devices from different manufacturers can communicate seamlessly. Well-known protocols include the Transmission Control Protocol (TCP), Internet Protocol (IP), Hypertext Transfer Protocol (HTTP), and Simple Mail Transfer Protocol (SMTP).

2.2.4 Interfaces

Network interfaces are the points of interaction between devices and the network. Each device has a network interface card (NIC) that facilitates connection to the network, enabling data transmission through the medium. These interfaces can be wired (Ethernet) or wireless (Wi-Fi).

2.3 Types of Network Communication

Network communication can be categorized into several types based on the mode of transmission, the scale of the network, and the nature of the communication.

2.3.1 Unicast, Broadcast, and Multicast

Unicast: In unicast communication, data is sent from one sender to one specific receiver. This is the most common form of communication on networks, exemplified by personal emails and direct file transfers.

Broadcast: Broadcast communication involves sending data from one sender to all possible receivers within a network segment. An example would be a local network announcement sent to all connected devices.

Multicast: Multicast allows data to be sent from one sender to multiple specified receivers simultaneously. This is commonly used for streaming video or audio to a group of users without overloading the network.

2.3.2 Peer-to-Peer vs. Client-Server

Peer-to-Peer (P2P): In a P2P network, each device (or peer) acts as both a client and a server, enabling direct communication and data sharing without central control. This architecture is common in file-sharing applications.

Client-Server: In client-server architecture, clients request resources or services from a centralized server, which processes these requests and returns the appropriate response. This model is used across many web applications and services.

2.4 The Network Layer Model

Understanding the different layers of network communication is crucial. The OSI (Open Systems Interconnection) model and the TCP/IP model are two widely recognized frameworks that illustrate the layers of network communication.

2.4.1 The OSI Model

The OSI model consists of seven layers:

Physical Layer: Deals with the hardware transmission of raw binary data over a medium.

Data Link Layer: Responsible for node-to-node data

transfer and error detection.

Network Layer: Manages routing and forwarding of data packets across the network.

Transport Layer: Ensures end-to-end communication and data integrity through error-checking and flow control.

Session Layer: Manages sessions and controls the dialogues between applications.

Presentation Layer: Transforms data formats and prepares data for the application layer.

Application Layer: Interfaces directly with end-user applications and provides network services to users.

2.4.2 The TCP/IP Model

The TCP/IP model simplifies networking into four layers:

Link Layer: Corresponds to the physical and data link layers of the OSI model.

Internet Layer: Equates to the OSI network layer and involves IP addressing.

Transport Layer: Similar to the OSI transport layer, focusing on reliable data transfer (TCP) and best- effort delivery (UDP).

Application Layer: Encompasses the functionality of the OSI's session, presentation, and application layers, dealing with end-user applications.

The fundamentals of network communication provide the building blocks for understanding more complex network scenarios. By comprehending devices, media, protocols, and the structure of network layers, one can gain insight into how data travels across networks and the technologies that enable our connected world.

How Data Packets Work at the Low Level

Understanding how these packets work at a low level requires an examination of the underlying protocols and assembly programming concepts that govern data manipulation and transfer at the machine level. This chapter dives deep into how data packets are formulated, transmitted, and processed in a network using assembly language, casting light on the interaction between hardware and software.

1. The Concept of Data Packets

Data packets are formatted units of data carried by packet-switched networks. Each packet contains not just the payload (the actual data being transmitted), but also metadata that provides routing information and control information. A typical packet structure includes:

Header: Contains source and destination IP addresses, a sequence number, and checksums for error-checking.

Payload: The actual data being sent from the sender to the receiver.

Trailer: Often used for error detection, such as a cyclic redundancy check (CRC). ## 2. The Role of the OSI Model

Before diving into assembly programming, it helps to refer to the Open Systems Interconnection (OSI) model, which provides a conceptual framework for how data packets travel through network layers.

Networking is divided into seven layers, from the physical layer (where binary data is converted to signals) up to the application layer (where end-user processes take place). Our focus will be primarily on the Data Link Layer (Layer 2) and the Network Layer (Layer 3), where much of the packet handling occurs.

3. Networking Hardware Basics ### 3.1 NIC (Network Interface Card)

At the heart of any networking system lies the Network Interface Card (NIC). This piece of hardware is responsible for generating and interpreting packet data. It handles the physical connection to the network and enables communication with other devices.

3.2 Microcontroller and Assembly

In some specialized networking applications, microcontrollers handle packet processing, often programmed in assembly language. Assembly language allows developers low-level control over hardware, providing the ability to write efficient code that directly interacts with the system's hardware resources.

4. Packet Structure at the Assembly Level

Using assembly language to work with data packets requires understanding how to structure and manipulate these packets in memory. Below is an example of defining a packet structure, demonstrating how to allocate memory and fill in the necessary fields.

4.1 Defining a Packet Structure These are typically defined as:

```assembly section .data
```

```
; Define packet structure

packet_size equ 64  ; Size of the packet

header_size equ 20 ; Default header size

; Packet structure

packet: db packet_size dup(0)    ; Reserve space for packet

; Packet fields

source_ip: db 4 dup(0)          ; 4 bytes for source IP
dest_ip: db 4 dup(0)        ; 4 bytes for destination IP

sequence_number: db 2 dup(0)        ; 2 bytes for sequence number payload: db 32 dup(0) ;  32 bytes for payload

trailer: db 4 dup(0) ; 4 bytes for error checking
```

In the above example, we define a packet with various fields in the `.data` section of our assembly program. ## 5. Sending a Packet

To send a packet, it primarily involves configuring the NIC to transmit data:

5.1 Preparing the Packet

We need to populate the packet's fields before transmission.

```assembly
mov byte [packet + 0], 192 ; Example source IP first byte
mov byte [packet + 1], 168 ; Example source IP second byte mov byte [packet + 2], 1    ; Example source IP
```

third byte mov byte [packet + 3], 1   ; Example source IP fourth byte

; Similarly fill in destination IP, sequence numbers, payload, etc.
```

### 5.2 Transmitting the Packet

Using system calls or interrupts (depending on the operating system being targeted), packets can be sent over the network. For example:

```assembly
; Assuming we use a hypothetical memory-mapped register for NIC mov eax, [NIC_SEND_REGISTER]

mov [eax], packet_address ; Store packet address to send it over the network
```

6. Receiving a Packet

Upon receiving a packet, the assembly code must handle it correctly: ### 6.1 Reading the Incoming Packet

Receiving data involves reading from specific registers or memory locations:

```assembly
mov ebx, [NIC_RECEIVE_REGISTER] ; Get the address of the new packet

; Process the packet fields

mov eax, [ebx + header_size] ; Read the header
```
```

; Continue processing the payload and trailer

```
```

6.2 Validating the Packet

After receiving the packet, checks like sequence numbers and checksums should be validated.

```assembly
; Example checksum verification call validate_checksum
```

Understanding how data packets work at a low level in assembly language involves a blend of knowledge about packet structure, NIC operation, memory management, and system calls. This foundational knowledge paves the way for more advanced networking operations and helps software engineers and developers create more efficient network-based applications. Mastery of these concepts is crucial for those wishing to work on network device firmware, embedded systems, or high-performance networking solutions.

Understanding Protocols: TCP/IP, UDP, and ICMP in Depth

This chapter delves into three fundamental protocols of the Internet Protocol Suite—TCP (Transmission Control Protocol), UDP (User Datagram Protocol), and ICMP (Internet Control Message Protocol). By understanding these protocols, you will gain insights into how devices communicate efficiently and reliably over networks.

The Internet Protocol Suite

31

The Internet Protocol Suite, commonly referred to as TCP/IP, is a set of communication protocols used for the Internet and similar networks. It is named after its two key protocols: TCP and IP (Internet Protocol). TCP/IP is layered into four abstraction layers:

Application Layer: Where user-level protocols reside (e.g., HTTP, FTP).

Transport Layer: Responsible for end-to-end communication protocols (TCP and UDP).

Internet Layer: Handles logical addressing and routing (IP).

Network Interface Layer: Deals with the physical transmission of data over the network.

This chapter focuses primarily on the Transport Layer, where TCP, UDP, and ICMP operate. ## TCP (Transmission Control Protocol)

TCP is a connection-oriented protocol that guarantees the reliable transmission of data across networks. It ensures that data packets arrive in order, without errors, and that all packets are received. The key features of TCP include:

1. Connection Establishment and Termination

TCP uses a three-way handshake mechanism to establish a connection. This process involves three steps:

SYN: The client sends a SYN packet to initiate a connection.

SYN-ACK: The server responds with a SYN-ACK packet, acknowledging the request and sending its own connection request.

ACK: The client sends an ACK packet, confirming the connection establishment. For connection termination, TCP utilizes a four-way handshake:

One side sends a FIN packet to indicate it has finished sending data.

The other side replies with an ACK before sending its own FIN packet.

The first side acknowledges the FIN with another ACK, completing the termination process. ### 2. Reliability and Error Detection

TCP accomplishes reliability through techniques such as:

Segmentation: Large messages are broken into smaller segments for transmission.

Acknowledgments (ACKs): The receiving device sends back an acknowledgment for received segments.

Retransmissions: If a segment is lost or an ACK is not received within a specified timeframe, TCP retransmits the segment.

Error detection is achieved using checksums, which verify the integrity of transmitted data. ### 3. Flow Control and Congestion Control

Flow Control prevents a sender from overwhelming a receiver by sending data faster than it can be processed. TCP employs a mechanism called the sliding window protocol, which allows multiple segments to be sent before needing an acknowledgment, while still keeping track of what has been acknowledged.

Congestion Control helps reduce network congestion by adjusting the rate of data transmission based on current network conditions. TCP employs algorithms like Slow Start and Congestion Avoidance to manage these adjustments.

UDP (User Datagram Protocol)

UDP is a connectionless protocol that provides a simpler, faster alternative to TCP, without the overhead of reliability features. It is used primarily in applications where speed is critical and some data loss is acceptable (e.g., video streaming, online gaming). Key features of UDP include:

1. Connectionless Communication

Unlike TCP, UDP does not establish a connection before sending data. Each packet, known as a datagram, is sent independently, and there is no guarantee of delivery or order. This reduces latency, making UDP ideal for real-time applications.

2. Lightweight and Fast

UDP has a smaller header size (8 bytes) compared to TCP (20 bytes), which means it incurs less overhead. This simplicity leads to faster transmission speeds, making it suitable for applications where real-time performance is critical.

3. No Congestion Control or Error Recovery

UDP does not provide built-in mechanisms for error checking, retransmissions, or flow control. If a packet is lost, it is up to the application layer to handle retransmission if needed. This is advantageous in scenarios where latency and speed are prioritized over reliability.

ICMP (Internet Control Message Protocol)

ICMP is a network layer protocol primarily used for diagnostic and error-reporting purposes, allowing devices to communicate network status and errors. While ICMP is not typically used for data exchange, it plays a pivotal role in managing IP network communication.

1. Error Reporting

ICMP reports errors that occur during packet processing. For instance, if a router cannot forward a packet due to a destination being unreachable, it sends back an ICMP Destination Unreachable message. Other common ICMP error messages include Time Exceeded (when a packet's time-to-live expires) and Parameter Problem (indicating issues with header fields).

2. Diagnostic Tools

ICMP is often used in network diagnostic tools like `ping` and `traceroute`:

Ping: Sends ICMP Echo Request messages to test the reachability of a host and measure round-trip time.

Traceroute: Sends ICMP Time Exceeded messages to determine the route packets take through the network by incrementally increasing the time-to-live value.

3. Control Messages

ICMP also includes control messages that help manage network operations and maintain performance. For instance, it can report on network congestion or provide information on redirecting traffic.

In summary, TCP, UDP, and ICMP are vital components of the Internet Protocol Suite, each serving distinct but complementary roles. TCP is designed for applications requiring reliable and ordered data delivery, while UDP offers a lightweight solution for speed-sensitive applications. ICMP provides essential error reporting and diagnostic capabilities that help maintain and troubleshoot networks.

Chapter 3: Working with Network Interfaces in Assembly

As systems grow more interconnected, the need to harness low-level programming skills to interact directly with network interfaces becomes vital for systems programmers, embedded developers, and anyone looking to optimize performance. This chapter delves into the low-level mechanisms for interfacing with network hardware using assembly language, providing insights into the architecture and principles that govern data transfer over networks.

3.1 Understanding Network Interfaces

A network interface controller (NIC) is a crucial component that enables communication between a computer and a network. It converts data into a format suitable for the transmission medium—be it wired, wireless, or optical—and vice versa. To interact with these interfaces at a low level, one must understand both the hardware and the software layers involved.

3.1.1 Types of Network Interfaces

There are various types of network interfaces, but the most commonly used in personal computers are Ethernet and Wi-Fi NICs. Each type has its specific protocols and modes of operation, yet the principles of interacting with them remain similar:

Ethernet: Utilizes standards like IEEE 802.3 and relies on the CSMA/CD (Carrier Sense Multiple Access with Collision Detection) protocol.

Wi-Fi (Wireless LAN): Operates under the IEEE

802.11 standards, which involve a higher level of complexity due to its handling of radio signals and wireless protocols.

Understanding these distinctions helps developers choose the right methods and instructions when programming network-related tasks, as different NICs may expose different registers and capabilities.

3.2 Setting Up the Environment

Programming in assembly language requires an appropriate development environment. In this chapter, we will assume the use of an x86 architecture, which is common in personal computers. Setting up your environment includes choosing an assembler (like NASM or GAS), a relevant operating system (Linux is preferred for network interface programming), and the necessary permissions since low-level networking tasks often require administrative rights.

3.2.1 Tools and Assemblers

NASM (Netwide Assembler): A popular assembler for x86 architecture known for its simplicity and portability.

GCC/GAS: Often used in combination with `gcc` for linking and additional functionalities within Unix/Linux systems.

3.2.2 Accessing Kernel Functions

To work with networking interfaces directly, you must interact with the operating system kernel. In Linux, this typically involves system calls for interfacing with sockets and driver layers abstracting NIC details. When direct access to hardware is required, developers can work with memory-mapped I/O that exposes the controller's registers.

3.3 Basic Networking Concepts

Before we dive into assembly programming, it's essential to understand some fundamental networking concepts, including:

IP Addressing: Identifying hosts on a network.

Socket Programming: Creating endpoints for sending and receiving data.

Protocols: TCP, UDP, and ICMP are essential for different types of communication. ### 3.3.1 Sockets

Sockets are the means by which data is sent and received over a network. In assembly, interacting with sockets may involve manipulating file descriptors and handling network byte order, but understanding the high-level abstraction is crucial to correctly implementing this at a low level.

3.4 Assembly Language Network Programming

In this section, we will write a simple assembly program to demonstrate how to interact with a network interface, creating a basic UDP client that sends a message to a predefined server. While other higher-level languages handle much of the complexity, understanding the assembly-level operations offers insights into data handling and packet creation.

3.4.1 Example: UDP Client in Assembly

```assembly
assembly section .data

msg db 'Hello, Network!', 0        ; Message to send
ip_address db 192, 168, 1, 1            ; Target IP
```

```
(Example) port dw 12345   ; Target Port
section .bss
socket_fd resd 1       ; File descriptor for socket
section .text global _start
_start:
; Create socket
mov eax, 102 ; syscall: socket
mov ebx, 2    ; AF_INET
mov ecx, 2    ; SOCK_DGRAM
xor edx, edx ; Protocol 0
int 0x80       ; Call kernel
mov [socket_fd], eax        ; Store socket fd
; Prepare the sockaddr_in structure
; (Fill in details as needed)
; Send message
mov eax, 104 ; syscall: sendto
; Prepare parameters to be passed (socket, msg, etc.)
; Close socket
mov eax, 6    ; syscall: close mov ebx, [socket_fd]
int 0x80       ; Call kernel
; Exit
mov eax, 1    ; syscall: exit
xor ebx, ebx  ; status 0
```

```
int 0x80      ; Call kernel
```
` ` `

3.4.2 Breakdown of the Example

Creating a Socket: The `socket` syscall is invoked to create a UDP socket, specifying the address family (IPv4) and type (UDP).

Preparing sockaddr_in Structure: This structure holds the destination address and port, which requires careful byte ordering.

Sending Data: The `sendto` syscall sends our predefined message to the target address and port.

Closing the Socket: Resource management is critical; hence, we need to close the socket after operations.

Exiting the Program: Ensuring a clean exit with the `exit` syscall. ## 3.5 Best Practices and Considerations

Error Handling: Every system call should have error checking after it is executed to handle any network-related issues.

Permissions: Direct network access might require elevated permissions; ensure the code runs under appropriate privileges.

Data Alignment: Beware of data alignment issues when passing structures to system calls.

Working with network interfaces in assembly provides a unique perspective on how data travels across the network and how applications interact with NIC hardware. By understanding the intricacies of network protocols and the low-level operations required, developers can create optimized and efficient networking applications.

Interacting with Network Adapters and Interfaces

This chapter aims to unravel the complexities of network programming using assembly, focusing on programming environments, architecture, and practical examples.

1. Understanding Network Adapters and Interfaces
1.1 What is a Network Adapter?

A network adapter, sometimes referred to as a network interface controller (NIC), enables a computer to connect to a network. It can be wired (like Ethernet) or wireless (like Wi-Fi) and is responsible for converting data from the computer into a format suitable for transmission over the network medium.

1.2 Network Interfaces

A network interface is the boundary point for connection between the user's computing device and the network. Different protocols exist for communication, including TCP/IP, UDP, and others. Each network interface is associated with a unique hardware address known as a MAC (Media Access Control) address.

2. Low-Level Networking: An Overview

Low-level networking involves using assembly language to directly manipulate hardware and interact with the operating system's network stack. This allows for optimized performance and tailored networking solutions, but it requires in-depth knowledge of both the assembly language and the specific architecture being used.

3. Programming Environment Setup

To work with network adapters in assembly, consider the following:

3.1 Tools Required

Assembler: A tool to convert assembly code into machine code (e.g., NASM, MASM).

Operating System: Familiarize yourself with the specific OS to understand system calls (Linux, Windows, etc.).

Network Adapter: Ensure you have access to a physical or virtual network adapter for experimenting.

3.2 Accessing Network Interfaces

Different operating systems provide varying methods for accessing network interfaces. In Linux, for instance, you could leverage system calls via the `/dev` hierarchy. On Windows, interactions typically occur through APIs that handle networking tasks.

4. Basic Assembly Language Constructs

Assembly language varies by architecture (x86, ARM, etc.), but fundamental constructs remain consistent across platforms:

Registers: Temporary storage in the CPU for quick data access.

Instructions: Assembly operation codes that the CPU executes.

Memory Management: Moving data from registers to memory and vice versa.

5. Writing Assembly Code for Networking

In this section, we will delve into sample assembly code

snippets. We will focus on an example of sending and receiving simple data packets over a network interface.

5.1 Setting Up the Environment

For our example, we will use a simple Linux environment with x86 assembly to interact with a TCP/IP socket.

Create a Socket: We will use the `socket()` system call to create a socket.

Bind the Socket: Use `bind()` to associate the socket with a local address and port.

Listen and Accept Connections: Set up the socket to listen for incoming connections using `listen()` and `accept()`.

5.2 Example Code

```assembly
assembly section .data

; Constants for socket creation socket_domain  equ 2  ; AF_INET

socket_type                equ 1                ; SOCK_STREAM protocol       equ 0  ; IPPROTO_TCP
addr_len                db 16          ; Address length
port    dw 8080        ; Port number

section .bss

sockfd resb 4 ;  Placeholder for socket file descriptor
client_addr resb 16       ; Client address structure

section .text global _start

_start:
; Create a socket
```

```
mov eax, 41   ; syscall: socket mov ebx, socket_domain
              ; domain mov ecx, socket_type              ;
type

mov edx, protocol              ; protocol int 0x80  ; Call  the
kernel

mov [sockfd], eax    ; Store the socket fd

; Bind the socket

; Load required values into registers as needed

; Listen on the socket

; Load required values into registers

; Accept a connection

; Load required values into registers

; Send or receive data

; Cleanup and exit

mov eax, 1     ; syscall: exit

xor ebx, ebx   ; status 0

int 0x80       ; Call the kernel
```

5.3 Explanation of Code

The above example outlines a rudimentary process for creating a socket. We create a TCP socket, bind it to a specific port, and get ready to listen for incoming connections. The actual send and receive handling will be performed next, utilizing similar system calls. The hardcoded constants establish parameters like address type and protocol.

6. Advanced Techniques

6.1 Direct Hardware Access

For more advanced operations, you may wish to directly manipulate network adapters through memory- mapped I/O, where you interact with the memory addresses mapped to your NIC.

6.2 Using Drivers

In modern systems, hardware abstraction and device drivers play vital roles. Assembly programming at this level may require loading kernel modules or interacting with existing drivers.

6.3 Using Interrupts

Understanding and using network interrupts can enhance performance by allowing the CPU to respond asynchronously to network events.

Interacting with network adapters and interfaces using assembly language is a rewarding but complex endeavor. With a firm grasp of assembly constructs, system calls specific to your operating system, and a good understanding of networking principles, you can leverage the power of assembly to create efficient and effective networking solutions.

Writing Assembly Code to Access Network Hardware

This chapter delves into writing assembly code to access network hardware, emphasizing the importance of low-level programming in networking contexts, understanding network architectures, and effectively interfacing with device drivers.

Understanding Network Hardware

Before diving into assembly code, it's crucial to understand the components that correspond to network hardware. At a high level, network hardware consists of:

Network Interface Cards (NICs): The hardware that connects computers to networks, including Ethernet and Wi-Fi cards.

Protocol Processors: Chips designed to handle specific networking protocols, enhancing performance.

Switches and Routers: Devices that route data between networks, performing complex switching and forwarding based on various algorithms.

Connectors and Cables: Physical mediums that carry data signals across distances.

Each of these components interfaces with the operating system through drivers, which abstract low-level hardware interactions.

The Role of Assembly Language

Assembly language is a low-level programming language that provides a symbolic representation of a computer's machine code instructions. While high-level programming languages offer easier syntax and abstractions, assembly programming allows direct manipulation of hardware resources, making it a powerful tool for performance-critical applications.

Advantages of Assembly Language in Networking

Efficiency: Assembly allows developers to write code that can execute faster than higher-level languages due to minimal abstraction and optimized machine-level instructions.

Memory Control: It provides fine-grained control over memory usage, which is crucial in network applications that require precise timing and management of buffers.

Hardware Access: Directly interacting with hardware registers and ports allows developers to optimize specific hardware features or handle unique hardware configurations.

Setting Up the Development Environment

Before writing assembly code, ensure that you have the following:

Assembler: An assembler converts assembly code into machine code, suitable for execution on hardware. Popular choices include NASM (Netwide Assembler) and GNU Assembler (GAS).

Emulator/Debugger: Tools like QEMU or Bochs, and debuggers such as GDB, help in testing and debugging assembly code without the risk of crashing the host system.

Network SDKs: Some hardware manufacturers provide Software Development Kits (SDKs) that include headers and additional libraries for interfacing with their devices.

Writing Assembly Code to Access Network Hardware
Communication with Network Interface Cards

To access a NIC, you will be primarily dealing with its memory-mapped I/O (MMIO) or using I/O ports. The network interface typically exposes a set of registers through which you can send and receive frames.

Example: Accessing a Network Card Register

Assuming you have a basic understanding of x86 assembly, below is a simplified example demonstrating how to read from and write to a register of a hypothetical Ethernet controller.

```assembly
section .data
```

; Define the base address for the network card's registers
nic_base dd 0xC0000000

section .text global _start

_start:

; Write a value to the NIC's command register to initialize it mov eax, 0x00000001   ; Command to initialize the NIC

mov ebx, [nic_base]; Load the base address of NIC into EBX mov [ebx + 0x00], eax   ;   Write   to command register (offset 0x00)

; Read the status register to check if the NIC is operational mov ecx, [nic_base + 0x04] ; Load the status register into

```
ECX cmp ecx, 0x00000001       ; Check if the NIC is
operational
jne .nic_error        ; If not, jump to error handling
; Further operations...
.nic_error:
; Handle NIC error (e.g., logging, light indication, etc.)
; ...
jmp _exit
_exit:
; Exit the program
mov eax, 1    ; syscall: exit
xor ebx, ebx  ; status: 0 int 0x80
```
` ` `

Configuring Network Protocols

After initializing network hardware, you generally need to configure it for specific protocols (like TCP/IP). Manipulating the Control and Status Registers (CSRs) as described in the technical reference for the network device can help in configuring parameters such as MAC address, MTU size, and more.

Handling Data Transmission

Data Buffers: Allocate and manage buffers in memory for sending and receiving packets.

Interrupts: Set up interrupts for handling incoming packets efficiently. This often involves writing to specific registers to enable interrupts for receive events.

Frame Formats: Ensure proper framing according to the networking protocol (Ethernet frames, IP packets, etc.) and compliance with protocol standards.

Example: Sending a Data Packet

Below is a conceptual outline for sending a packet, using assembly language with respect to the registers of the NIC used for we assume Ethernet:

```assembly
; Preparing an Ethernet Frame section .data

source_mac db 0x00, 0x1A, 0x2B, 0x3C, 0x4D, 0x5E
destination_mac db 0xFF, 0xFF, 0xFF, 0xFF, 0xFF, 0xFF
ethertype db 0x08, 0x00 ; IP protocol

section .text send_packet:

; Fill the frame buffer (in DS:DX) with the Ethernet frame
mov [buffer], destination_mac

mov [buffer + 6], source_mac mov [buffer + 12], ethertype

; Fill in the payload...

; Send the frame to the NIC

mov eax, buffer       ; Get the buffer address

mov ebx, [nic_base]; Load the base address of the NIC

mov [ebx + 0x10], eax        ; Assume 0x10 is the offset for the "send" register

; Add necessary steps for ensuring the packet is sent
```

Debugging and Testing

Debugging assembly code can be challenging due to its low-level nature, making use of an emulator or a debugger essential. Techniques include:

Step through instructions: Observe register states and memory.

Breakpoints: Set breakpoints at critical junctures, especially before and after hardware operations.

Logging: Print debug messages to external logging systems or within the program wherever feasible.

By understanding the hardware's registers, protocols, and how to manipulate them directly, developers can optimize performance and efficiency, leading to better overall network throughput and reliability.

Chapter 4: Socket Programming in Assembly

This chapter delves into socket programming using Assembly language, focusing on the x86 architecture under the Linux operating system.

4.1 Understanding Sockets

A socket is an endpoint for sending or receiving data across a computer network. It offers a way for applications to communicate within a system or across different systems. Sockets are created using the socket API, which provides functions to create sockets, bind them to ports, listen for incoming connections, send or receive data, and close connections.

Types of Sockets:

Stream Sockets (TCP): Provide reliable, connection-oriented communication.

Datagram Sockets (UDP): Offer connectionless communication without guaranteed delivery. ## 4.2 Socket API Overview

The socket API is a set of functions provided by the operating system to create and manage sockets. Below are some fundamental functions we will explore in this chapter:

`socket()`: Create a new socket.

`bind()`: Bind a socket to an address and port.

`listen()`: Listen for incoming connections (for TCP).

`accept()`: Accept an incoming connection.

`connect()`: Connect to a remote socket.

`send()`: Send data over a socket.

`recv()`: Receive data from a socket.

`close()`: Close a socket.

4.3 Setting Up the Environment

Before diving into socket programming in Assembly, you need a suitable development environment. Here's a quick guide for setting up a Linux environment with NASM (Netwide Assembler):

Install NASM: This is the assembler needed to convert Assembly language code into machine code.

```bash
sudo apt-get install nasm
```

Install GCC: While we will be focusing on Assembly, having GCC installed will be helpful for linking.

```bash
sudo apt-get install build-essential
```

Create a Development Directory: Organize your code files.

```bash
mkdir socket_example cd socket_example
```

4.4 Creating a Simple TCP Server

Let's explore how to create a simple TCP server using Assembly language. This server will:

Create a socket.

Bind it to a port.

Listen for connections.

Accept a connection.

Receive a message.

Send a response.

Close the connection. ### 4.4.1 TCP Server Code

Here's the Assembly code to create a simple TCP server:

```assembly
section .data

ip_addr db '127.0.0.1' ; IP address port dw 8080    ; Port number msg db 'Hello from server!', 0

section .bss

sockfd resd 1       ; Socket file descriptor client_sock resd 1              ; Client socket file descriptor addr resb 16      ; Address buffer

msg_buffer resb 256      ; Message buffer

section .text global _start

_start:
; Create socket

; int socket(int domain, int type, int protocol) mov eax, 102    ; syscall: socket

mov ebx, 2   ; AF_INET

mov ecx, 1   ; SOCK_STREAM
```

```asm
xor edx, edx   ; protocol = 0
int 0x80       ; call kernel
mov [sockfd], eax    ; store socket descriptor
; Bind socket
; struct sockaddr_in addr
; int bind(int sockfd, const struct sockaddr *addr,
socklen_t addrlen) mov eax, dword [sockfd]
mov ebx, addr        ; pointer to the struct sockaddr mov
dword [ebx], 2                ; sin_family = AF_INET mov
word [ebx + 2], port         ; sin_port = port
mov dword [ebx + 4], 0   ;        sin_addr.s_addr     =
INADDR_ANY mov ecx, 16        ; size of struct sockaddr
int 0x80       ; call kernel
; Listen for connections
; int listen(int sockfd, int backlog)


mov eax, 104 ; syscall: listen mov ebx, dword [sockfd]
mov ecx, 5     ; backlog
int 0x80       ; call kernel
; Accept connection
; int accept(int sockfd, struct sockaddr *addr, socklen_t
*addrlen) mov eax, 114    ; syscall: accept
mov ebx, dword [sockfd]
xor ecx, ecx   ; no address
xor edx, edx   ; no address length
```

```
int 0x80        ; call kernel
mov [client_sock], eax      ; store client socket descriptor
; Receive message
; int recv(int sockfd, void *buf, size_t len, int flags) mov
eax, 102        ; syscall: recv
mov ebx, dword [client_sock]
mov ecx, msg_buffer             ; pointer to buffer mov
edx, 256        ; buffer length
xor edi, edi    ; flags = 0
int 0x80        ; call kernel
; Send message
; int send(int sockfd, const void *buf, size_t len, int flags)
mov eax, 103 ; syscall: send
mov ebx, dword [client_sock]
mov ecx, msg; pointer to message
mov edx, 20   ; message length
xor edi, edi    ; flags = 0
int 0x80        ; call kernel
; Close socket
; int close(int fd)
mov eax, 6      ; syscall: close mov ebx, dword [client_sock]
int 0x80        ; call kernel
; Exit program
mov eax, 1      ; syscall: exit
```

```
xor ebx, ebx   ; status = 0
int 0x80        ; call kernel
```
```

### 4.4.2 Explanation of Key Sections

**Creating a Socket**: The server creates a new socket with the `socket()` syscall.

**Binding**: The server binds to the specified port using the `bind()` syscall, setting the necessary fields in the address structure.

**Listening**: The server listens for incoming connections using the `listen()` syscall.

**Accepting Connections**: With `accept()`, the server waits for a client to connect and receives a new socket descriptor for communication.

**Receiving and Sending Data**: The server can receive data from the client and send a response using

`recv()` and `send()` syscalls.

**Closing the Connection**: Finally, it closes the connection with `close()`. ## 4.5 Creating a Simple TCP Client

Next, we will create a TCP client that connects to the server, sends a message, and waits for a response. ### 4.5.1 TCP Client Code

Here's the Assembly code for the TCP client:

```assembly section .data

ip_addr db '127.0.0.1' ; IP address port dw 8080       ; Port number msg db 'Hello, server!', 0
```

58
```

```
section .bss

sockfd resd 1 ; Socket file descriptor

addr resb 16  ; Address buffer msg_buffer resb 256
    ; Message buffer

section .text global _start

_start:

; Create socket

mov eax, 102 ; syscall: socket

mov ebx, 2    ; AF_INET

mov ecx, 1    ; SOCK_STREAM

xor edx, edx  ; protocol = 0

int 0x80      ; call kernel

mov [sockfd], eax   ; store socket descriptor

; Connect to server

; struct sockaddr_in addr mov eax, dword [sockfd]

mov ebx, addr       ; pointer to struct sockaddr mov
dword [ebx], 2    ; sin_family = AF_INET mov word [ebx
+ 2], port   ; sin_port = port

mov dword [ebx + 4], 0    ;        sin_addr.s_addr    =
inet_addr(ip_addr) mov ecx, 16   ; size of struct sockaddr

mov eax, 104          ; syscall: connect int 0x80 ;        call
kernel

; Send message

mov eax, 103 ; syscall: send mov ebx, dword [sockfd]

mov ecx, msg; pointer to message
```

```
mov edx, 20  ; message length
xor edi, edi  ; flags = 0
int 0x80      ; call kernel
; Receive response
mov eax, 102 ; syscall: recv mov ebx, dword [sockfd]
mov ecx, msg_buffer          ; pointer to buffer mov
edx, 256      ; buffer length
xor edi, edi  ; flags = 0
int 0x80      ; call kernel
; Close socket
mov eax, 6    ; syscall: close mov ebx, dword [sockfd]
int 0x80      ; call kernel
; Exit program
mov eax, 1    ; syscall: exit
xor ebx, ebx  ; status = 0
int 0x80      ; call kernel
```
```

### 4.5.2 Explanation of Key Sections

**Creating a Socket**: The client similarly uses `socket()` to create a new socket.

**Connecting to the Server**: The client connects to the server using the `connect()` syscall, specifying the server's address and port.

**Sending and Receiving Data**: The client sends a message and then waits for a response.
```

Closing the Connection: Finally, the `close()` syscall closes the socket. ## 4.6 Compiling and Running the Programs

To compile and run your socket programs, use the following commands in the terminal:

Compile the Server:

```bash
nasm -f elf32 -o server.o server.asm gcc -m32 -o server server.o
```

Run the Server:

```bash
./server
```

Compile the Client:

```bash
nasm -f elf32 -o client.o client.asm gcc -m32 -o client client.o
```

Run the Client:

```bash
./client
```

Make sure to run the server first and then run the client to establish the connection.

We learned about the key syscalls used for socket operations and how data flows between the client and server. Understanding these low-level details enhances your comprehension of network programming and equips you with the necessary tools to work in more complex environments.

Creating and Managing Sockets with System Calls

In this chapter, we will delve into the creation and management of sockets using system calls in assembly language. While higher-level languages like C simplify socket programming, assembly provides deep insights into the mechanics of system calls and network communication.

1. Understanding Sockets

Before we dive into the assembly code, it is vital to understand what a socket is. A socket is an endpoint for sending and receiving data across a network. It allows two machines to communicate over a network using standard protocols, mainly TCP (Transmission Control Protocol) and UDP (User Datagram Protocol).

1.1 Types of Sockets

Stream Sockets (SOCK_STREAM): These provide reliable, connection-oriented communication. They use TCP as the transport layer.

Datagram Sockets (SOCK_DGRAM): These support connectionless, unreliable communication using UDP.

1.2 Protocol Families

AF_INET: This address family is used for IPv4 addresses.

AF_INET6: This address family is used for IPv6 addresses. ## 2. Essential System Calls for Socket Programming

In UNIX-like systems, several system calls are vital for socket programming:

`socket()`: To create a new socket.

`bind()`: To assign an address to the socket.

`listen()`: To prepare a socket to accept incoming connections (used for server sockets).

`accept()`: To accept a connection from a client.

`connect()`: To connect to a server socket.

`send()`, `recv()`: To send and receive data over the socket. ## 3. Setting Up the Environment

Before proceeding with assembly socket programming, ensure that you have the following:

A Linux environment (such as Ubuntu).

An assembler like NASM.

Local network access (for testing socket communication).

4. Writing Assembly Code

This section outlines the assembly code required to create and manage sockets. We will write a basic TCP server that listens for incoming connections.

4.1 Creating a Socket

```assembly
`` `assembly section .data

sockfd resd 1 ; Variable to hold socket file descriptor
addr_in sockaddr_in            ; Structure to hold address info

port dw 8080        ; Port number, 8080 ip db '127.0.0.1',
0        ; Localhost IP address

section .text global _start

_start:

; Create a socket with PF_INET family, SOCK_STREAM
type, and 0 protocol mov eax, socket(AF_INET,
SOCK_STREAM, 0)

mov [sockfd], eax    ; Save the socket descriptor

; Prepare sockaddr structure

mov dword [addr_in.sin_family], AF_INET mov word
[addr_in.sin_port],      htons(port)      mov      dword
[addr_in.sin_addr], inet_addr(ip)

; Bind the socket
```

```
mov ebx, [sockfd]    ; Load socket descriptor into ebx mov
ecx, addr_in ; Load  address  of  sockaddr_in  mov edx,
sizeof sockaddr_in  ; Size of sockaddr structure mov eax,
bind(ebx, ecx, edx)
```

; Listen for incoming connections

```
mov eax, listen(ebx, 5)      ; Max 5 queued connections
```

; Accept a connection

```
mov ebx, [sockfd]    ; Load  socket  descriptor  mov ecx,
addr_in       ; Pointer to sockaddr_in
```

```
mov edx, sizeof sockaddr_in      ; Size can be NULL for
the server mov eax, accept(ebx, ecx, edx) ; Accept the
connection
```

; Connection accepted successfully

; Here you can implement further communication logic
```
` ` `
```

4.2 Binding and Listening

The binding process connects the socket to a specific IP address and port number, allowing it to listen for incoming connections. The listening setup prepares the server for incoming requests.

4.3 Accepting Connections

The `accept()` call waits for clients to connect to the listening socket. Upon a successful connection, it returns a new socket descriptor for the accepted connection, enabling communication with the client.

5. Sending and Receiving Data

Once a connection is established, you can use `send()` and `recv()` to manage data transmission.

```assembly
section .text
; Loop to send and receive data data db 'Hello, World!', 0
message resb 256    ; Buffer to hold incoming messages
send_receive:
; Send data to the connected client
mov eax, send(new_sockfd, data, strlen(data), 0)
; Receive data from the client
mov eax, recv(new_sockfd, message, sizeof(message), 0)
; Process received message
```

6. Closing the Socket

Finally, remember to close the sockets when they are no longer needed. Use the `close()` system call for this purpose.

```assembly
; Close server socket mov eax, close(sockfd)
; Close accepted connection mov eax, close(new_sockfd)
```

While writing socket code in assembly can be more complex and verbose than in higher-level languages, it provides a deeper understanding of the underlying processes involved in network communication. With this foundation, you can build more sophisticated network applications directly in assembly, tapping into the low-level capabilities of your operating system.

Writing a Simple TCP and UDP Socket in Assembly

Socket programming is a fundamental aspect of networking, allowing programs to communicate over a network. This chapter explores the implementation of simple TCP and UDP sockets using Assembly language, which provides a low-level interface to the operating system's networking capabilities. Assembly programming can be complex and requires a solid understanding of the underlying architecture and system calls. In this chapter, we will use the x86 architecture and Linux system calls for our examples.

Understanding Sockets

Before we dive into the code, let's understand what sockets are. A socket is an endpoint for communication between two machines or processes. TCP (Transmission Control Protocol) sockets provide reliable, connection-oriented communication, while UDP (User Datagram Protocol) sockets offer a simpler, connectionless communication method. Both protocols have their use cases, and understanding how to implement them in Assembly is crucial for low-level programming tasks.

Assembly Language Basics

Assembly language is a low-level programming language that is specific to a computer architecture. It offers direct control over hardware and system resources, making it ideal for system programming but requiring precise instruction coding. For our examples, we will be using

NASM (Netwide Assembler) syntax for x86 architecture, which is commonly used in Linux environments.

The Linux Networking API

Linux provides a robust set of system calls for socket programming. The most important ones for our purposes are:

`socket()`: Creates a new socket.

`bind()`: Binds a socket to a local address and port.

`listen()`: Prepares a socket to accept incoming connections (TCP only).

`accept()`: Accepts an incoming connection (TCP only).

`connect()`: Initiates a connection to a remote socket (TCP only).

`send()`: Sends data over a socket.

`recv()`: Receives data from a socket.

`sendto()`: Sends data to a specific address (UDP only).

`recvfrom()`: Receives data from a specific address (UDP only).

`close()`: Closes a socket.

Let's walk through the implementation of a simple TCP server and a UDP client. ## Implementing a Simple TCP Server

TCP Server Code

Below is a simple Assembly language program that creates a TCP server. The server listens for incoming connections and sends a greeting message to the client.

```assembly
section .data
message db "Hello from TCP Server", 0 message_len equ $ - message
port dw 8080
section .bss sockaddr resb 16
sockfd resd 1
newsockfd resd 1
section .text global _start
_start:
; Create socket
mov eax, 102 ; sys_socket mov ebx, 2     ; AF_INET
mov ecx, 1    ; SOCK_STREAM mov edx, 0       ; Protocol
int 0x80
mov [sockfd], eax
; Bind socket
mov eax, 104 ; sys_bind mov ebx, [sockfd]
; Prepare sockaddr_in
mov dword [sockaddr], 2  ;    AF_INET    mov   word [sockaddr + 2], port ; Port
mov dword [sockaddr + 4], 0 ; INADDR_ANY
mov ecx, 16 ; Length of sockaddr int 0x80
; Listen on socket
mov eax, 106 ; sys_listen mov ebx, [sockfd]
```

```
mov ecx, 5    ; Backlog int 0x80
; Accept incoming connection mov eax, 105 ; sys_accept
mov ebx, [sockfd]
xor ecx, ecx mov edx, 0 int 0x80
mov [newsockfd], eax
; Send message
mov eax, 103 ; sys_send mov ebx, [newsockfd] mov ecx,
message
mov edx, message_len
int 0x80
; Close sockets
mov eax, 6    ; sys_close mov ebx, [newsockfd] int 0x80
mov ebx, [sockfd] int 0x80
; Exit program
mov eax, 1    ; sys_exit xor ebx, ebx
int 0x80
```
```

### Explanation

**Create Socket**: The `socket()` system call creates a new socket for TCP communication.

**Bind Socket**: The `bind()` system call associates the socket with a local address and port.

**Listen**: The socket is prepared to accept incoming connections with `listen()`.

**Accept Connection**: The `accept()` system call waits
```

for a client to connect, returning a new socket for the connection.

Send Message: A greeting message is sent to the connected client using the `send()` system call.

Cleanup: Finally, the sockets are closed, and the program exits. ## Implementing a Simple UDP Client

UDP Client Code

Now, let's implement a simple UDP client that sends a message to a server.

```assembly
section .data
```

message db "Hello from UDP Client", 0 message_len equ $ - message

port dw 8080

ip_address db "127.0.0.1"

section .bss sockaddr resb 16

sockfd resd 1

section .text global _start

_start:

; Create socket

mov eax, 102 ; sys_socket mov ebx, 2   ; AF_INET

mov ecx, 2   ; SOCK_DGRAM mov edx, 0

int 0x80

mov [sockfd], eax

; Prepare sockaddr_in

71

```
mov dword [sockaddr], 2   ;   AF_INET   mov   word
[sockaddr + 2], port        ; Port

mov dword [sockaddr + 4], ip_address   ; IP Address

; Send message

mov eax, 112 ; sys_sendto mov ebx, [sockfd]

mov ecx, message  mov edx, message_len  mov esi,
sockaddr mov edi, 16

int 0x80

; Close socket

mov eax, 6   ; sys_close mov ebx, [sockfd]

int 0x80

; Exit program

mov eax, 1   ; sys_exit xor ebx, ebx

int 0x80

```
```

Explanation

Create Socket: Similar to the TCP server, we create a UDP socket using the `socket()` system call.

Prepare Address: A `sockaddr_in` structure is prepared with the IP address and port number for the message destination.

Send Message: The `sendto()` system call is used to send the message to the specified address without establishing a connection.

Cleanup: The socket is closed, and the program exits.
```

By implementing a simple TCP server and a UDP client, we learned how to create sockets, bind them to addresses, and send data. While Assembly programming may seem daunting due to its complexity and low- level nature, mastering it empowers developers to work closely with hardware and optimize applications for performance.

Chapter 5: Packet Manipulation and Injection

Understanding how to manipulate packets at a low level — using assembly language—provides unique insights into the functioning of network protocols and can be instrumental for developers, network engineers, and security researchers alike.

Assembly language, being a low-level programming language, allows us to interface directly with hardware and system resources. This chapter will delve into the concepts of packet manipulation and injection, focusing on how assembly can be utilized to create, modify, and send packets over a network.

Foundations of Networking Protocols

Before diving into the mechanics of packet manipulation, it's important to understand the structure of network packets and protocols. At its core, a packet is a formatted unit of data carried by a packet-switched network. This unit consists of two main components:

Header: Contains metadata such as source and destination IP addresses, protocol type, and other control information.

Payload: The actual data being transmitted.

Commonly used network protocols include TCP (Transmission Control Protocol), UDP (User Datagram Protocol), and ICMP (Internet Control Message Protocol). Each has a standardized header structure that must be adhered to for successful transmission and reception.

Setting Up the Environment

To manipulate network packets using assembly language, we must set up an appropriate development environment. This typically involves:

Assembler: A tool that converts assembly language code into machine code for execution.

Network Library Support: In some cases, you may need bindings or libraries that allow assembly code to interface with networking stacks of the operating system.

On Linux systems, you'll often work with system calls to interact with the network stack. For instance, the

`socket`, `bind`, `sendto`, and `recvfrom` system calls will be your primary tools for creating and sending packets.

Basic Packet Creation

In assembly, we can create a simple IP or UDP packet. This requires understanding the structure of the packet headers:

IPv4 Header Structure

An IPv4 header consists of various fields, including:

Version (4 bits)

Header Length (4 bits)

Type of Service (8 bits)

Total Length (16 bits)

Identification (16 bits)

Flags (3 bits)

Fragment Offset (13 bits)

Time to Live (8 bits)

Protocol (8 bits)

Header Checksum (16 bits)

Source Address (32 bits)

Destination Address (32 bits)

This can be visualized in assembly as a series of bytes laid out in memory. #### Example Code: Creating a Simple UDP Packet (in NASM Syntax)

```assembly
section .data
```

; Define the IP addresses and payload src_ip db 192, 168, 1, 10 ; Source IP

dst_ip db 192, 168, 1, 20 ; Destination IP payload db 'Hello, Network!', 0 ; Data

section .text global _start

_start:

; Create socket

; Using syscall number for socket(AF_INET, SOCK_DGRAM, 0) mov rax, 41   ; syscall: socket

mov rdi, 2   ; AF_INET

mov rsi, 2   ; SOCK_DGRAM xor rdx, rdx   ; protocol 0 syscall

; Socket file descriptor in rax; save it mov rdi, rax   ; socket fd

```
; Prepare IP header
; [Details for header omitted for brevity]
; Populate header fields such as source and destination IPs

; Prepare UDP header
; [Details for header omitted for brevity]
; Populate UDP fields (length, checksum, etc.)

; Send packet using syscall
; Using syscall number for sendto mov rax, 44   ;    syscall: sendto
; Arguments setup: fd, buffer address, length, flags, addr pointer syscall

; Exit
mov rax, 60          ; syscall: exit xor rdi, rdi    ; status 0
syscall
```
` ` `

Packet Injection Techniques

Packet injection is the process of sending crafted packets onto a network to test devices, analyze responses, or exploit vulnerabilities. With the basics of creating a packet outlined, we can utilize tools like `libpcap` or write kernel modules for more sophisticated tasks.

Raw Sockets

Creating raw sockets allows the assembly program direct access to the network layer, enabling the crafting and injection of arbitrary packets. This involves setting appropriate socket options and ensuring you have the required permissions.

Example Code: Packet Injection (Pseudo)

```assembly
; Set socket options for raw socket (if needed)
; Configure IP_HDRINCL for raw IP packet mov rax, 54
    ; setsockopt syscall
; [setuparguments] syscall
; Build IP header (as shown earlier)
; Generate UDP (or TCP) header
; Inject packet using 'sendto' as shown previously
```

Practical Applications of Packet Manipulation

Understanding packet manipulation can be invaluable in several scenarios:

Security Assessments: Tools such as Metasploit rely on packet manipulation to exploit network services.

Network Testing: Validate the robustness of firewall rules by sending packets that are expected to be blocked.

Protocol Development: Test custom implementations of protocols by observing responses to unique packet constructions.

By understanding and practicing these methods, network

practitioners can gain deeper insights into network behavior and enhance their skills in network security, analysis, and development.

Constructing and Modifying Network Packets Manually

In this chapter, we delve into the intricate process of constructing and modifying network packets using assembly language. By understanding the low-level data manipulation, you will gain insights into how networking protocols operate under the hood, and you will develop skills to create or modify packets for various purposes such as network debugging, penetration testing, or developing custom protocols.

Understanding Network Protocols

Before diving into assembly language, it is essential to understand the fundamental concepts of network protocols. Common protocols include:

TCP (Transmission Control Protocol): Ensures reliable, ordered, and error-checked delivery of data.

UDP (User Datagram Protocol): A simpler interface, providing connectionless communication with no guarantee of delivery.

IP (Internet Protocol): Responsible for routing packets across networks.

Each of these protocols has a specific structure and set of rules governing how data is packaged and transmitted.

Knowledge of these structures forms the basis for packet construction.

Packet Structure

A network packet typically consists of:

Header: Contains metadata such as source and destination IP addresses, protocol types, and control flags.

Payload: The actual data being transmitted.

Trailer (optional): May include error-checking information like checksums.

For the sake of demonstration, we will focus on an IP packet with a TCP segment, as these are widely used on the internet.

Assembly Language Basics

Assembly language serves as a bridge between high-level programming languages and machine code. It's specific to computer architectures, meaning that code written for one type of CPU architecture (like x86) will not run on another (like ARM) without modification.

Before we start constructing packets, familiarize yourself with basic assembly operations:

Registers: Small storage locations within the CPU that hold data temporarily.

Instructions: Commands that tell the CPU what operations to perform.

Memory Management: Understanding how to allocate, access, and modify memory. ## Crafting the Packet

To illustrate the process of manually constructing a network packet, we will focus on creating a minimal TCP packet encapsulated in an IP packet.

Step 1: Setting Up Your Environment You will need:

An assembler (such as NASM for x86).

A network sniffer (like Wireshark) to inspect packets.

Root or administrative access to allow raw packet manipulation. ### Step 2: Defining the Packet Structure

The first step is to define the structure of our packet. Below are brief outlines for TCP and IP packet structures:

IP Header Structure (20 bytes):

```

Version (4 bits) | IHL (4 bits) | Type of Service (1 byte) | Total Length (2 bytes) | Identification (2 bytes) | Flags (3 bits) | Fragment Offset (13 bits) |

TTL (1 byte) | Protocol (1 byte) | Header Checksum (2 bytes) | Source IP (4 bytes) | Destination IP (4 bytes)

```

TCP Header Structure (20 bytes):

```

Source Port (2 bytes) | Destination Port (2 bytes) |

Sequence Number (4 bytes) | Acknowledgment Number (4 bytes) | Data Offset (4 bits) | Reserved (3 bits) | Flags (9 bits) |

Window Size (2 bytes) | Checksum (2 bytes) | Urgent Pointer (2 bytes) | Options (variable length)

81
```

```
```

Step 3: Writing the Assembly Code

Let's write an assembly routine that constructs a simple packet. The code snippet below illustrates creating an arbitrary IP/TCP packet:

```assembly
assembly section .data

; Define packet buffers

ip_header db 0, 0, 0, 0, 0, 0, 0, 0, 0, 0, 0, 0, 0, 0, 0, 0, 0, 0, 0, 0

tcp_header db 0, 0, 0, 0, 0, 0, 0, 0, 0, 0, 0, 0, 0, 0, 0, 0, 0, 0, 0, 0

section .text global _start

_start:

; Construct IP header

mov byte [ip_header], 0x45          ; Version and IHL

mov word [ip_header + 2], 0x003C    ; Total Length (60 bytes)

mov dword [ip_header + 12], 0xC0A80001 ; Source IP (192.168.0.1) mov dword [ip_header + 16], 0xC0A80002 ; Destination IP (192.168.0.2)

; Construct TCP header

mov word [tcp_header], 0x1F90   ; Source Port (8136)

mov word [tcp_header + 2], 0x1F91       ; Destination Port (8137)
```

```
mov dword [tcp_header + 4], 0    ; Sequence number

mov dword [tcp_header + 8], 0    ;        Acknowledgment
number mov byte [tcp_header + 12], 0x50              ;
Data offset

; Additional TCP flags and other fields should be filled
similarly

; ... Code to send this packet raw over the network

; Exit

mov eax, 1    ; syscall: exit

xor ebx, ebx  ; exit status 0 int 0x80
```
```

### Step 4: Sending the Packet

Executing this code will construct your packet. However, to send raw packets, you would typically use system calls or socket programming APIs. In assembly, it's common to interface with lower-level network APIs or manipulate raw sockets to send the packets you've manually constructed.

## Modifying Existing Packets

To modify packets, you can capture existing packets using a library like `libpcap` in C or build your capturing mechanism using assembly. Once captured, you can dissect the packets, modify the headers or payloads directly in memory, and then re-inject these packets back into the network.

Constructing and modifying network packets manually in assembly is a profound way to understand the fundamental workings of computer networking. Through this process, you can develop skills applicable in various
```

fields, from network security and troubleshooting to developing custom low-level applications.

Using Assembly to Inject Custom Packets into the Network

This chapter explores how to leverage Assembly language for the purpose of injecting custom packets, allowing you to manipulate network traffic, test security, and understand the underlying protocols.

1. Understanding Packet Injection

Packet injection involves generating and transmitting custom packets onto a network interface. This practice can serve multiple purposes, including performance testing, protocol analysis, and vulnerability assessments. Tools like `Scapy` in Python and `hping` in C are frequently used for packet crafting, yet Assembly language provides a lower-level approach that grants complete control over the network stack.

1.1 Why Assembly?

Using Assembly language for packet injection offers several advantages:

Precision: Assembly gives you meticulous control over the binary data sent over the network.

Performance: Assembly code can be highly optimized for speed, allowing for efficient processing.

Learning Opportunity: Writing Assembly enhances your understanding of system architecture and networking principles.

1.2 Basic Networking Concepts

Before diving into packet injection using Assembly, it's crucial to understand some basic networking concepts such as:

Protocol Layers: Understand the OSI model and where packet injection operates (typically at Layer 3 - Network Layer and Layer 4 - Transport Layer).

Packet Structure: Familiarize yourself with the structure of common packets (Ethernet, IP, TCP, UDP).

Raw Sockets: To inject packets, you will often need to use raw sockets, which bypass the standard TCP/IP stack.

2. Setting up Your Environment

To get started with packet injection in Assembly, you'll need a suitable development environment: ### 2.1 Choose Your Operating System

Most packet injection tasks are performed on UNIX-like systems such as Linux. A Linux distribution provides the necessary tools and supports raw socket operations in Assembly.

2.2 Required Tools

Compiler/Assembler: Use `gcc` for compiling C code or `nasm` for assembling Assembly code.

Network Tools: Install `libpcap` or equivalent libraries for packet capturing and analysis.

Development Libraries: Link against necessary libraries for socket programming if needed. ## 3. Writing Assembly Code for Packet Injection Let's delve into a basic example of how to create a simple TCP packet injector with Assembly. This example will send a TCP SYN packet to a specified target, initiating a connection.

3.1 The Assembly Code

```assembly
section .data

ip_target db '192.168.1.10' ; Target IP address

eth_header                                    db
0x00,0x0C,0x29,0x3D,0x2C,0x26,0x00,0x00,0x00,0x00
,0x00,0x00 ; Dummy Ethernet header

ip_header                                     db
0x45,0x00,0x00,0x28,0x00,0x00,0x40,0x00,0x40,0x06
; Initial part of IP header

section .bss sockfd resd 1

packet resb 1500      ; Buffer for the packet

section .text global _start

_start:

; Create raw socket

mov eax, 102 ; syscall: socket

mov ebx, 2    ; AF_INET

mov ecx, 6    ; SOCK_RAW int 0x80

mov [sockfd], eax    ; Save socket descriptor

; Prepare the packet

; Fill in Ethernet header, IP header, and TCP header here...

; Assemble complete packet into the 'packet' buffer

; Send packet
```

```
mov eax, 104 ; syscall: sendto mov ebx, [sockfd]
    ; socket descriptor
```

; Other parameters like target address and buffer to send...
int 0x80

; Close socket

```
mov eax, 6    ; syscall: close mov ebx, [sockfd]
```

int 0x80

; Exit

```
mov eax, 1    ; syscall: exit xor ebx, ebx
```

int 0x80
```
```

3.2 Explanation of the Code

Socket Creation: The `socket` syscall creates a raw socket that enables packet manipulation.

Packet Construction: The assembly code defines a basic structure for the Ethernet and IP headers. You would need to complete the packet by adding TCP header fields and the payload.

Sending the Packet: The `sendto` syscall transmits the constructed packet through the created socket.

Cleanup: After sending the packet, the socket is closed, and the program exits gracefully. ## 4. Compiling and Running the Code

Once the code is written, compile and run it using the

following commands:

```bash
nasm -f elf32 -o injector.o injector.asm gcc -m32 -o injector injector.o

sudo ./injector
```

Ensure you run the program with elevated privileges (using `sudo`) since raw socket operations require it. ## 5. Considerations and Ethics

5.1 Legal Aspect

Always conduct packet injection in a controlled environment or on networks where you have permission to execute such actions. Unauthorized access to networks or systems is illegal and unethical.

5.2 Network Impact

Be aware that injecting malicious packets can disrupt services and lead to network instability. Use these techniques responsibly.

5.3 Learning and Experimentation

Packet injection can be a powerful tool for network troubleshooting and learning. Always prioritize ethical guidelines and digital responsibility when using such skills.

Injecting custom packets into a network using Assembly provides a foundational understanding of how networking operates at a fundamental level. Through this process, engineers and researchers can not only develop practical skills but also gain insight into the intricacies of network protocols and security.

Chapter 6: TCP/IP Protocol Implementation in Assembly

The Transmission Control Protocol (TCP) and Internet Protocol (IP)—commonly referred to as TCP/IP—are the foundational protocols of the Internet. They dictate how data is packetized, addressed, transmitted, and received across networks. The implementation of TCP/IP in assembly language presents unique challenges and opportunities, providing insights into low-level networking and system design.

In this chapter, we will delve into the modularity of TCP/IP, focusing on how these comprehensive protocols can be broken down and implemented in assembly language. We will explore the functions of each layer, provide examples of assembly code for specific operations, and discuss the implications and intricacies of managing network communication at such a low level.

1. Understanding TCP/IP Protocol Stack The TCP/IP model is organized into four layers:

Link Layer (Network Interface Layer): This layer is responsible for the physical transmission of data over a specific medium (e.g., Ethernet, Wi-Fi). It handles framing and addressing tasks.

Internet Layer: This layer manages the logical addressing and routing of packets across multiple networks. IP operates at this level.

Transport Layer: Here, TCP and UDP work to ensure

reliable (TCP) and unreliable (UDP) communication across the network.

Application Layer: This is where end-user applications operate, using the services provided by the transport layer.

In our implementation, we will focus on functionalities in the Internet and Transport layers. ## 2. Environment Setup

Before we start coding, we need to set up an appropriate environment. We suggest using an x86 assembly language assembler/debugger, such as NASM (Netwide Assembler), along with access to a virtual machine that can mimic a network environment.

Basic setup requires:

A supported operating system (e.g., Linux)

NASM installed for assembling our code

Necessary permissions to manage network interfaces ## 3. The Internet Layer: IP Implementation

The Internet Layer is where the IP protocol resides, responsible for addressing and routing packets. Here's how we can manage IP packet structuring in assembly language.

3.1. Structuring IP Packets

An IP packet consists of a header and payload. The header includes important information such as the version, header length, total length, source address, and destination address.

Here is an example of setting up an IP packet header in

assembly:

```assembly
section .data

ip_header db 0          ; Version and IHL (Internet
Header Length) db 0     ; Type of Service

dw 0   ; Total Length

dw 0   ; Identification

dw 0x4000  ; Flags and Fragment Offset db 255        ;
Time To Live

db 6   ; Protocol (TCP) dw 0              ;        Header
Checksum

dd 0   ; Source IP (to be set)

dd 0   ; Destination IP (to be set)

section .text global _start

_start:

; Code to set source and destination IP addresses

; Code to calculate the IP header checksum
```

3.2. Building and Sending Packets

To send packets over a network, we need to use system calls to access network interface devices. In Linux, you can use sockets.

```assembly
; Using syscall to create a socket mov eax, 102        ;
syscall: socket mov ebx, 2   ; domain: AF_INET
```

91

mov ecx, 1 ; type: SOCK_STREAM mov edx, 0   ; protocol: IPPROTO_IP int 0x80 ; Call kernel

; Save the socket descriptor for further operations mov [socket_fd], eax

``` ` ` ` ```

4. The Transport Layer: TCP Implementation

The Transport layer is where TCP resides, ensuring reliable data transmission. ### 4.1. Establishing TCP Connections

TCP operates using a three-way handshake method to establish a connection. #### SYN Packet Creation

Following the IP packet creation, you will prepare a TCP packet:

```assembly section .data```

tcp_header db 0x0 ; Source Port (to be filled) db 0x0 ; Destination Port (to be filled)

``` ` ` ` ```

dw 0x0000 ; Sequence Number

dw 0x0000 ; Acknowledgment Number db 0x50   ; Data Offset

db 0x02   ; Flags (SYN) dw 0x0000 ; Window Size dw 0x0000 ; Checksum

dw 0x0000 ; Urgent Pointer
```

4.2. Sending TCP Packets

To send a TCP packet, it typically involves filling out appropriate headers and using the socket system call:

```assembly
; Assuming ip_header and tcp_header are prepared:

mov eax, 104 ; syscall: sendto

mov ebx, [socket_fd]              ; socket descriptor mov ecx, ip_header      ; pointer to buffer

mov edx, size_of_packet  ; size of the packet to send mov esi, 0  ; flags

int 0x80      ; Call kernel
```

5. Handling Incoming Packets

Receiving packets and processing them involves using sockets to listen on defined ports and protocols. You can use the `recv` syscall to fetch incoming data.

```assembly
; Listening for incoming connections mov eax, 102    ; syscall: socket

; ... (setup code as before)

; Assuming we've bound the socket to an address and port

; Now listen for incoming connections. mov eax, 104   ; syscall: listen

mov ebx, [socket_fd]       ; socket descriptor mov ecx, 5    ; backlog

int 0x80      ; Call kernel
```

```
; Accepting a connection
mov eax, 106 ; syscall: accept
mov ebx, [socket_fd]        ; socket descriptor
; (Getting client address setup) int 0x80 ; Call kernel
` ` `
```

Implementing TCP/IP protocols in assembly language offers an unparalleled look into the intricacies of networking. While assembly programming can be complex and the development time considerable, it enhances understanding of how protocols function at their core.

We explored the essential building blocks for implementing the Internet Protocol (IP) and Transmission Control Protocol (TCP) using assembly language. The meticulous nature of assembly language programming offers robust advantages, particularly in embedded systems and high-performance applications, where system resources are limited.

Building a Basic TCP Handshake in Assembly

The TCP handshake is a three-step process that establishes a connection between a client and a server before data transmission begins. In this chapter, we will delve into the fundamentals of the TCP handshake and explore how to implement it using Assembly language. While working with Assembly provides a low-level perspective, it also requires a good understanding of network programming concepts.

Understanding the TCP Handshake

Before we dive into the implementation, let's briefly review the three stages of the TCP handshake:

SYN - The client sends a SYN (synchronize) packet to the server to initiate the connection.

SYN-ACK - The server responds with a SYN-ACK (synchronize-acknowledge) packet, acknowledging the receipt of the client's SYN packet.

ACK - The client sends an ACK (acknowledge) packet back to the server to confirm receipt of the SYN-ACK packet, completing the handshake.

Once this handshake is complete, a reliable connection is established, and data can be transmitted. ## Environment Setup

To work with Assembly language for network communication, we need an appropriate environment. We will be using Linux, as it provides system calls for socket programming that we can access via Assembly language. You will need:

A Linux-based operating system.

An Assembly language assembler (like NASM).

A networked environment (real or virtual) to perform the TCP handshake. ## Socket Programming Basics

Before jumping into Assembly, it is important to understand how sockets work. In a typical C program for TCP communication, the following steps are taken:

Create a Socket: Using `socket()`.

Bind the Socket: Using `bind()` for servers.

Listen for Connections: Using `listen()` for servers.

Accept Connections: Using `accept()` for servers.

Connect to a Server: Using `connect()` for clients.

Send and Receive Data: Using `send()` and `recv()`.

Using these concepts as our foundation, we'll look into how to replicate this in Assembly language. ## Implementing the TCP Handshake in Assembly Language

Creating the Client

In this section, we will write an Assembly program that creates a TCP client that performs the TCP handshake.

```assembly
section .data
ip_address db '127.0.0.1', 0          ;      Server      IP
address port dw 12345     ; Port number

sockfd db 0   ; Socket file descriptor

section .bss

sockaddr resb 16     ; Space for sockaddr structure

section .text global _start


_start:
; Create a socket
mov eax, 102 ; sys_socket

mov ebx, 2   ; AF_INET

mov ecx, 1   ; SOCK_STREAM
```

```asm
xor edx, edx   ; Protocol 0
int 0x80       ; Call kernel
mov [sockfd], eax    ; Store the socket fd
; Prepare sockaddr_in structure
; 16 bytes for sockaddr, which contain:
; sin_family (2 bytes) + sin_port (2 bytes) + sin_addr (4
bytes) + sin_zero (8 bytes)
; Fill it out
mov dword [sockaddr], 2   ;    AF_INET    mov    word
[sockaddr + 2], port      ; Port
mov dword [sockaddr + 4], dword [ip_address]  ; IP
address (127.0.0.1) sub eax, eax   ; Zero out eax
; Connect to the server
mov eax, 104 ; sys_connect
mov ebx, [sockfd]    ; Socket fd
mov ecx, sockaddr                 ; Pointer to sockaddr
mov edx, 16          ; Length of sockaddr int 0x80   ;
Call kernel
; If connection is successful, we can send data or proceed
; For demonstration, let's send a simple message.
; Close the socket
mov eax, 6           ; sys_close mov ebx, [sockfd]
            ; Socket fd int 0x80 ; Call kernel
; Exit gracefully
mov eax, 1   ; sys_exit
```

```
xor ebx, ebx   ; Exit code 0

int 0x80        ; Call kernel
```
```
### Key Sections Explained

**Creating a Socket**: We use the `sys_socket` system call to create a TCP socket.

**Preparing the sockaddr Structure**: The sockaddr structure is filled with the server's IP address and port number in the appropriate byte order.

**Connecting to the Server**: The `sys_connect` system call is invoked to establish a connection to the server, completing the TCP handshake.

### Compiling and Running

To compile and run this program, you will need to save it as `tcp_client.asm`, and then follow these steps in your terminal:

```bash
nasm -f elf32 -o tcp_client.o tcp_client.asm ld -m elf_i386 -o tcp_client tcp_client.o

./tcp_client  # Make sure a server is running on the specified port
```

Building the Server (Optional)

While the focus of this chapter is on the client-side TCP handshake, creating a simple server can help validate the
```

handshake. A similar approach can be taken for the server using `sys_bind`, `sys_listen`, and

`sys_accept` system calls.

We explored how to implement a basic TCP handshake using Assembly language by creating a simple client application. We discussed the underlying concepts of TCP and socket programming and demonstrated the Assembly implementation for creating a TCP client that initiates the handshake with a server.

Handling TCP Segments and Flags Programmatically

Understanding how to handle TCP segments and manipulate flags programmatically at an assembly language level is crucial for low-level network programming and systems design. In this chapter, we will explore the structure of a TCP segment, examine the meaning and purpose of various TCP flags, and demonstrate how to work with them in assembly language.

TCP Segment Structure

A TCP segment is structured as follows:

Source Port (16 bits)

Destination Port (16 bits)

Sequence Number (32 bits)

Acknowledgment Number (32 bits)

Data Offset (4 bits)

Reserved (3 bits)

Flags (9 bits)

Window Size (16 bits)

Checksum (16 bits)

Urgent Pointer (16 bits)

Options (variable length)

Data (variable length)

The flags field consists of several control bits that dictate the TCP connection's behavior. These flags include SYN (Synchronize), ACK (Acknowledgment), FIN (Finish), RST (Reset), PSH (Push), and URG (Urgent).

TCP Flags

SYN: Initiates a connection.

ACK: Acknowledges receipt of a segment.

FIN: Terminates a connection.

RST: Resets a connection.

PSH: Asks to push the buffered data to the receiving application.

URG: Indicates that the segment contains urgent data.
Understanding TCP Flags in Assembly

To manipulate TCP segments and flags, we first need to understand how to define the TCP segment structure in assembly language, manage the flags, and handle operations such as setting, clearing, and checking these flags.

Defining TCP Segment Structure in Assembly

In a typical assembly language, we might define the TCP structure using `struct` in higher-level assembly languages or a similar concept in the flat memory model of x86 assembly. Here's an example of how we might define a TCP segment in a common assembly language:

```asm
; Define TCP Segment structure TCP_Segment struc
```

Source_Port dw ? Destination_Port   dw   ?
Sequence_Number   dd   ?
Acknowledgment_Number dd ? Data_Offset   db ?

Reserved   db 0

Flags db ? Window_Size   dw ?

Checksum   dw ? Urgent_Pointer
    dw ? Options db 40 dup(?)

Data   db 1460 dup(?) TCP_Segment ends
```
```

In this structure, the `Flags` field can be manipulated directly as a byte. ### Setting TCP Flags in Assembly

To set a specific flag, we can use bitwise operations. For instance, to set the SYN flag, we need to modify the appropriate bit in the `Flags` byte. Let's consider that the SYN flag is the first bit (0x02):

```asm
; Set SYN flag
```

mov al, [tcpSegment.Flags]

or al, 0x02   ; Set the SYN flag mov [tcpSegment.Flags], al

```
```

Clearing TCP Flags in Assembly

Similarly, we can clear a flag using bitwise AND and negation. To clear the SYN flag, we would do the following:

```asm
; Clear SYN flag

mov al, [tcpSegment.Flags]

and al, 0xFD ; Clear the SYN flag (0xFD is 0b11111101) mov [tcpSegment.Flags], al
```

Checking TCP Flags in Assembly

To check if a specific flag is set, we can use the bitwise AND operation:

```asm
; Check if the SYN flag is set mov al, [tcpSegment.Flags]

and al, 0x02 ; Check the SYN flag jz no_syn   ; Jump if not set (zero)

; Flag is set; perform action no_syn:
```

Handling TCP Segments within Applications

To create an application that sends TCP segments, you must integrate these manipulations with the rest of your networking stack. This involves preparing the TCP segment, calculating the checksum, and interfacing with the network stack to send your segment over the network.

Example: Sending a TCP Segment

```asm
; Example pseudo-code for sending a TCP segment section
.data

tcpSegment TCP_Segment <...initialize fields...>

section .text

_start:
; Prepare TCP segment
; Set flags
call set_tcp_flags
; Calculate checksum call calculate_checksum
; Send the TCP segment call send_tcp_segment
set_tcp_flags:
; Set SYN flag
mov al, [tcpSegment.Flags] or al, 0x02
mov [tcpSegment.Flags], al ret
calculate_checksum:
; Implement checksum calculation logic ret
send_tcp_segment:
; Implement the logic to send the segment over the
network ret
```

We have delved into the process of handling TCP segments and flags programmatically using assembly language. By defining the TCP segment structure and employing bitwise operations to manipulate TCP flags, we gain full control over TCP communication at a low level.

Chapter 7: UDP Communication and Raw Sockets

UDP is a connectionless protocol that facilitates low-latency and low-overhead communication, making it particularly useful for real-time applications such as video streaming, online gaming, and Voice over IP (VoIP). Raw sockets, on the other hand, provide a means to handle low-level network operations, allowing for complete control over the packet structure and protocol used for transmission.

Understanding how to implement UDP communication and manipulate raw sockets in assembly will provide invaluable insights into network programming and systems-level operations.

7.1 Overview of UDP Protocol

UDP is a transport layer protocol defined in RFC 768. Unlike its counterpart, Transmission Control Protocol (TCP), UDP does not guarantee message delivery, order, or duplicate protection. Instead, it offers a simple way to send and receive datagrams—independent packets of data.

Features of UDP

Connectionless: There is no need to establish a connection before data transfer.

Lightweight: No overhead from establishing and maintaining a connection, making it faster than TCP.

Unreliable: Packets may arrive out of order, be duplicated, or be lost without notification. ### Use Cases

UDP is commonly used in scenarios where speed is critical

and occasional data loss is acceptable, such as:

Video conferencing

Online gaming

DNS lookups

Live broadcasting

7.2 Understanding Raw Sockets

Raw sockets allow programmers to access the underlying protocol layers directly. This enables custom implementations of protocols and detailed crafting of the packet structure. Raw sockets can send and receive packets without relying on any higher-level transport protocols, such as TCP or UDP.

Potential Uses of Raw Sockets

Building custom protocols

Custom packet sniffing tools

Network debugging

Security analysis and forensics ## 7.3 Setting Up the Environment

Before diving into assembly code for UDP communication and raw sockets, ensure that you have a suitable development environment. For assembly programming on Linux:

Install an assembler: Use NASM (Netwide Assembler).

Set up a Linux environment: Any contemporary distribution will suffice, but ensure you have the necessary headers and libraries for network programming. ## 7.4

UDP Communication in Assembly

7.4.1 Creating a UDP Socket

The first step in establishing UDP communication is creating a socket using the `socket` system call. Below is an example in x86-64 assembly:

```asm
section .data

domain dd 2 ; AF_INET for IPv4

type    dd 2    ; SOCK_DGRAM for UDP protocol dd 0
                ; IPPROTO_UDP

section .text global _start

_start:

; Create the socket

mov rax, 41   ; syscall: socket mov rdi, [domain]       ; domain mov rsi, [type]      ; type

mov rdx, [protocol] ; protocol syscall

mov rsi, rax   ; save the socket descriptor

; Further socket operations (bind, sendto, recvfrom) will follow...
```

7.4.2 Binding to a Port

Next, you need to bind the socket to an address and port number. This is done using the `bind` system call.

```asm
section .data

sockaddr_in:

.ss_family dw 2      ; AF_INET
```

.sin_port dw 0x1234   ; Port number in network byte order

.sin_addr dd 0   ; Listening on all interfaces

section .text

; Bind the socket

mov rax, 49   ; syscall: bind

mov rdi, rsi   ; socket descriptor lea rsi, [sockaddr_in]   ; address to bind

mov rdx, 16   ; size of sockaddr struct syscall

```

### 7.4.3 Sending and Receiving Data

To send and receive data, utilize the `sendto` and `recvfrom` system calls. The following snippet shows how to send a message.

```asm section .data

msg db 'Hello, UDP!', 0

section .text

; Send a message

mov rax, 44   ; syscall: sendto

mov rdi, rsi   ; socket descriptor lea rsi, [msg]    ; message buffer mov rdx, 12        ; message length

mov r10, sockaddr_in       ; destination address mov rdx, 16     ; size of address

syscall

```
```

Receiving data follows a similar structure, utilizing the `recvfrom` syscall to read incoming packets. ## 7.5 Raw Socket Communications

To create raw sockets, the steps are similar but will require elevated privileges (running as root). Below is a simple demonstration of creating a raw socket.

```asm
section .data
raw_type dd 3       ; SOCK_RAW for raw socket

section .text

; Create a raw socket
mov rax, 41    ; syscall: socket mov rdi, [domain]          ; domain mov rsi, [raw_type]              ; type
mov rdx, 0     ; protocol syscall
```

7.5.1 Crafting Packets

When using raw sockets, you'll need to construct the packet manually. Here's an outline of building an ICMP echo request packet:

```asm
section .data
icmp_header:
.type    db 8   ; ICMP type (Echo Request)
.code    db 0   ; Code
.checksum    dw 0   ; Checksum (set later)
.id      dw 1   ; Identifier
.sequence  dw 1     ; Sequence Number
```

section .text

; Fill in packet details and send using sendto as shown previously.

```
```

7.5.2 Listening for Incoming Packets

Use the `recv` system call to read incoming packets:

```asm
; Receive a packet
mov rax, 66   ; syscall: recv
mov rdi, rsi   ; socket descriptor
lea rsi, [buffer]        ; buffer to hold incoming packet mov rdx, BUFFER_SIZE ; size of buffer
syscall
```

Though working directly with assembly can be laborious due to its low-level nature, it allows for unparalleled control over the network stack. Understanding these mechanisms lays the groundwork for building efficient, high-performance network applications.

Implementing a UDP Client and Server in Assembly

Unlike TCP, UDP does not establish a connection before

110

data transmission and does not guarantee that packets will arrive in the same order they were sent. This makes UDP suitable for applications like gaming, live video streaming, and VoIP, where speed is critical, and some packet loss is acceptable.

In this chapter, we will explore how to implement a basic UDP client and server using Assembly language. This implementation will serve as an introduction to network programming at a low level, demonstrating how to utilize system calls for sending and receiving data over the network.

Prerequisites

Before diving into the implementation, ensure you have a basic understanding of the following concepts:

Assembly Language: Familiarity with basic assembly syntax and operations.

Networking Fundamentals: Understanding of UDP, sockets, and IP addressing.

Operating System Interfaces: Knowledge of system calls and how to interface with the operating system for network communication.

Environment Setup

We will use Linux as the operating system for this implementation, as it provides straightforward access to system calls for socket programming. Make sure you have an assembler such as NASM (Netwide Assembler) installed, along with a command-line interface for compiling and running assembly programs.

UDP Server Implementation ### Step 1: Initialize the

Socket

The first step in creating a UDP server is to create a socket with the appropriate parameters.

```assembly section .data
sockaddr_in:          ; Struct for socket address (family, port, address) family       dw 2   ; AF_INET

port    dw 8888      ; Port number

address              dd 0   ; Wildcard IP address (INADDR_ANY) zero       db 0, 0, 0, 0 ; Zero padding if needed

section .text global _start

_start:

; Create socket (AF_INET, SOCK_DGRAM, 0) mov eax, 102            ; socket syscall number mov ebx, 2      ; AF_INET

mov ecx, 2    ; SOCK_DGRAM

xor edx, edx  ; Protocol

int 0x80      ; Call kernel


mov esi, eax  ; Store socket descriptor
```

Step 2: Bind the Socket

Next, bind the socket to the specified port and address.

```assembly
; Bind socket
```

```
mov eax, 104        ; bind syscall number mov ebx, esi;
```
socket descriptor

```
lea ecx, [sockaddr_in]  ; pointer to sockaddr_in struct
mov edx, 16  ; size of sockaddr_in
```

```
int 0x80        ; Call kernel
```
` ` `

Step 3: Receive Data

Now we can implement a loop to receive incoming UDP packets.

` ` `assembly receive_loop:

; Prepare buffer

; Buffer to store incoming data

```
rx_buffer db 1024    ; Buffer size of 1024 bytes
```

; Receive from socket

```
mov eax, 109          ; recvfrom syscall number mov ebx,
esi    ; socket descriptor
```

```
lea ecx, [rx_buffer] ; buffer to store data mov edx, 1024
        ; buffer length
```

```
xor edi, edi    ; no flags
```

```
lea rsi, [sockaddr_in]        ; pointer to client's addr mov
r8d, 16        ; client address length
```

```
int 0x80        ; Call kernel
```

; Process received data (e.g., print to console or respond)

; (omitting the print function for brevity)

```
jmp receive_loop    ; Repeat to continue receiving
```

```
```

Step 4: Cleanup

We would also need to implement cleanup instructions to close the socket gracefully when the server shuts down.

```assembly
; Close socket
mov eax, 6    ; close syscall number
mov ebx, esi  ; socket descriptor
int 0x80      ; Call kernel
```

UDP Client Implementation ### Step 1: Create a Socket

Similar to the server, we start the client by creating a socket.

```assembly
section .text global _start

_start:
; Create socket (AF_INET, SOCK_DGRAM, 0) mov eax, 102
mov ebx, 2    ; AF_INET
mov ecx, 2    ; SOCK_DGRAM
xor edx, edx  ; Protocol int 0x80
mov esi, eax  ; Store socket descriptor
```

Step 2: Prepare and Send Data

The client needs to specify the server's address and port when sending data.

```assembly
; Prepare server address server_addr:
family        dw 2  ; AF_INET port      dw 8888
    ; Server port

address       dd [desired_ip_address] ; Server IP address


; Prepare data to send
tx_buffer db 'Hello, UDP Server!', 0
; Send to server

mov eax, 103        ; sendto syscall number mov ebx, esi
    ; socket descriptor

lea ecx, [tx_buffer]        ; pointer to data mov edx, 20
    ; data length

lea rsi, [server_addr] ; pointer to server address mov r8d,
16      ; address length

int 0x80      ; Call kernel
```

Step 3: Cleanup

Similar to the server, the client will also need code to close the socket when finished.

```assembly
; Close socket
mov eax, 6    ; close syscall number
```

```
mov ebx, esi  ; socket descriptor
int 0x80      ; Call kernel
` ` `
```

We established a socket, bound it to an address, and set up a simple loop for receiving packets on the server side. The client is capable of sending messages to the server. This implementation serves as an excellent primer into the world of low-level networking, providing insight into how data is transmitted over the network using UDP.

Sending and Receiving Raw Packets Using Assembly

In this chapter, we will explore the principles and procedures involved in sending and receiving raw packets using assembly language, delving into essential concepts such as socket programming, raw packet manipulation, and the intricacies of network protocols.

Understanding Raw Packets

Raw packets bypass the higher-level protocols typically handled by the operating system and allow access to the network layer. This is particularly useful for developing applications that require custom network protocols, packet sniffing, or network analysis. Operators need to understand the structure of IP packets, TCP/UDP headers, and how data fits within these frameworks.

Packet Structure

116

A basic packet consists of the following components:

Header: Contains metadata such as source and destination IP addresses and other routing information.

Payload: The actual data being sent across the network.

Checksum: A value used for error checking.

For our purposes, we will focus on IP packets with an emphasis on the headers and the required information for creating and interpreting them.

Setting Up the Environment

Before we can start programming, you will need an x86 assembly programming environment. This includes:

An assembler (e.g., NASM or MASM)

A Linux or Windows environment with raw socket capabilities

Root or administrative access to create and manage raw sockets ### Building the Assembly Environment

Install Needed Tools: Use package managers such as `apt` for Ubuntu or `brew` for macOS to install your assembler.

Configure Permissions: On Unix-like systems, you may need to grant your user account permission to create raw sockets. This is typically done via `sudo` or running your program as the root user.

Creating Raw Sockets ### Socket Creation

The first step in sending and receiving raw packets is to create a socket. In assembly language, this can be accomplished using system calls. Here is a simplified example of how to create a raw socket in x86 assembly for Linux.

```assembly
section .data
sockfd dd 0  ; Stores the socket file descriptor protocol dd 0 ; Protocol can be set to 0 for default

section .text global _start

_start:
; Create raw socket with AF_INET (IPv4) and SOCK_RAW
mov eax, 102 ; syscall: socket

mov ebx, 2    ; AF_INET

mov ecx, 3              ; SOCK_RAW mov edx, protocol
        ; protocol int 0x80   ; Call kernel
; Store the socket file descriptor mov [sockfd], eax

; Further code to send/receive packets goes here

; Exit program

mov eax, 1    ; syscall: exit

xor ebx, ebx  ; status 0 int 0x80
```

Error Handling

When creating a socket, it is essential to handle errors properly. If the system call fails, the register `eax` will contain a negative value. You should implement checks immediately following the socket creation to handle any failures gracefully.

Sending Raw Packets

To send raw packets, you must construct the packet first, which includes filling in the headers. Below is a basic approach to preparing and sending an IP packet.

Constructing the Packet

A typical IP packet includes the following fields:

Version and IHL: Indicating the version of the IP protocol and the header length.

Total Length: The total length of the packet.

Identification, Flags, and Fragment Offset: Used for packet fragmentation.

TTL (Time to Live), Protocol: For routing what type of packet it is.

Source and Destination Address.

Here's a simplified packet framework in assembly:

```
```assembly section .bss

packet resb 60        ; Allocate space for the packet


section .text global _start

; Other parts of the code remain unchanged...
construct_packet:

mov [packet.version_ihl], 0x45 ; IPv4, header length 20 bytes (5 * 4)

mov word [packet.total_length], 0x003c ; Total length field, e.g., 60 bytes

; Set other fields...
```
```

; Fill IP addresses, etc.

; Send packet

send_packet:

; Prepare to send the packet

mov eax, 130 ; syscall: sendto mov ebx, [sockfd]
         ; socket fd mov ecx, packet   ; buffer to send

mov edx, 60   ; length of the packet mov esi, 0   ; flags

; Address structure provided for sendto

; The rest of sendto params should be set

int 0x80   ; Call kernel
```

### Address Structures

The `sendto` system call requires an address structure that contains the destination address. You will need to create this structure separately, often in the `.data` section.

## Receiving Raw Packets

Receiving raw packets is similar but requires a different system call and handling:

```assembly recv_packet:

mov eax, 131 ; syscall: recvfrom mov ebx, [sockfd]
         ; socket fd

```
mov ecx, packet   ; buffer to store received packet
mov edx, 60 ; size of the buffer

mov esi, 0   ; flags

; Address structure for recvfrom int 0x80   ;   Call
kernel
```
` ` `

### Parsing Received Packets

Once a packet is received, you can parse it similarly to how you constructed it, addressing fields based on the expected structure defined above.

By creating and parsing raw packets, developers can implement advanced networking applications, conduct security research, or analyze network protocols at a low level.

# Chapter 8: Low-Level Data Encryption for Secure Communication

This chapter explores low-level data encryption techniques specifically designed for secure communication in network applications, utilizing assembly language.

## 8.1 Fundamentals of Data Encryption

Data encryption transforms plaintext into ciphertext to prevent unauthorized access to sensitive information. The main goals of encryption include:

**Confidentiality**: Ensuring that only authorized entities can access the original data.

**Integrity**: Verifying that the data has not been altered during transmission.

**Authentication**: Confirming the identity of the sender and receiver of the message.

Common encryption algorithms fall into two categories: symmetric-key and asymmetric-key encryption. Symmetric-key encryption uses the same key for both encryption and decryption, while asymmetric-key encryption utilizes a pair of keys—public and private.

## 8.2 Assembly Language for Low-Level Encryption

Assembly language allows for granular control over system resources, which can lead to optimizations that are not feasible in high-level languages. Below are some key advantages of utilizing assembly language for encryption routines:

**Performance**: Assembly language can produce highly

optimized code that runs faster than interpreted or compiled high-level languages, which is crucial for time-sensitive applications like network communications.

**Hardware Access**: With assembly language, developers can directly manipulate CPU registers and instructions, enabling low-level optimizations such as minimizing memory access.

**Portability and Compatibility**: Assembly code can be tailored to specific hardware configurations, ensuring that encryption routines execute efficiently across different architectures.

## 8.3 Overview of Encryption Algorithms

### 8.3.1 Advanced Encryption Standard (AES)

AES is a widely used symmetric encryption algorithm that operates on blocks of data. It employs a key size of 128, 192, or 256 bits. The algorithm consists of several rounds of processing, including substitution, permutation, mixing, and key addition.

### 8.3.2 Data Encryption Standard (DES)

DES is an earlier symmetric encryption standard that operates on 64-bit blocks using a 56-bit key. Although it has largely been superseded by AES due to vulnerabilities, understanding its operations can provide insights into implementing encryption in assembly.

### 8.3.3 Rivest Cipher (RC4)

RC4 is a stream cipher known for its simplicity and speed. While now considered less secure for modern applications, it serves as an example of implementing encryption with minimal resource consumption, an essential aspect when dealing with low-level programming.

## 8.4 Implementing AES in Assembly Language

Implementing AES in assembly requires a deep understanding of the algorithm's structure. The key steps involve:

### 8.4.1 Key Expansion

The first step is to generate a set of round keys from the main encryption key. This involves using the Rijndael key schedule to create a series of keys to be used in each round of encryption.

```assembly
; Pseudo-code for key expansion key_expansion PROC

; Expand the original key into round keys

; Implementation specifics will depend on the target architecture RETURN

key_expansion ENDP
```

8.4.2 Encryption Rounds

AES consists of multiple rounds (10, 12, or 14, depending on key size). Each round involves four operations: SubBytes, ShiftRows, MixColumns, and AddRoundKey.

```assembly
; Pseudo-code for AES encryption round aes_encrypt_round PROC

CALL SubBytes CALL ShiftRows CALL MixColumns
```

CALL AddRoundKey RETURN

aes_encrypt_round ENDP

```
```

8.4.3 Final Round

The final round omits the MixColumns step and concludes with SubBytes, ShiftRows, and AddRoundKey.

```assembly
; Pseudo-code for final round of AES aes_final_round PROC

CALL SubBytes CALL ShiftRows CALL AddRoundKey RETURN

aes_final_round ENDP
```

8.4.4 Decryption

Decryption in AES requires reversing the encryption steps, ensuring that every operation is appropriately inverted.

8.5 Secure Communication Protocols

No encryption system operates in isolation. Secure communication protocols, such as Transport Layer Security (TLS), utilize encryption algorithms to provide a secure channel over the internet. When implementing encryption in assembly, it is vital to consider how to integrate with these protocols for effective security.

8.6 Coding Best Practices

When writing low-level encryption routines in assembly, developers should keep the following best practices in mind:

Test Thoroughly: Encryption routines must be rigorously tested against known vectors to ensure correctness.

Avoid Hardcoding Keys: Security practices recommend against hardcoding encryption keys into source code.

Use Safe Memory Practices: Be cautious with memory allocation and deallocation, and avoid exposing sensitive data in memory.

8.7 Challenges in Low-Level Encryption

While low-level encryption can yield performance benefits, it also poses challenges:

Complexity: Writing and maintaining low-level assembly code can be more error-prone than high- level languages.

Portability: Assembly routines may not be easily portable across different processors or operating systems.

Security Risks: The lowest-level control can inadvertently introduce vulnerabilities if not handled correctly.

Low-level data encryption is a powerful approach to secure communication, particularly for applications demanding high performance and granular hardware control. While the complexity of working in assembly language can be daunting, the benefits in efficiency and resource management make it a valuable skill for systems developers.

Implementing XOR and Basic Encryption in Assembly

This chapter explores how to implement the XOR operation and basic encryption techniques using assembly language. By the end of this chapter, you will have a solid understanding of how to perform these operations at a low level, which will form the basis for more advanced encryption techniques.

Understanding XOR

The XOR operation is a binary operation that takes two bits as input and produces a single output bit. The output is true (1) if the inputs are different and false (0) if they are the same. The truth table for the XOR operation is as follows:

A	B	A XOR B
---	---	
0	0	0
0	1	1
1	0	1
1	1	0

In cryptography, XOR is often used because of its reversible nature: applying the XOR operation twice with the same key returns the original data.

Setting Up the Environment

Before we delve into the implementation, ensure you have

the necessary tools. For assembly programming on modern systems, you may use assemblers like NASM or MASM and a debugging tool like GDB.

Here's a brief overview of setting up NASM:

Install NASM: You can download it from [nasm.us](https://www.nasm.us/).

Write your assembly code: Use any text editor to create your `.asm` file.

Assemble the code: Use the command `nasm -f elf64 filename.asm` to produce an object file.

Link the object file: You can link the object file using `ld -o output filename.o`.

Run the executable: Execute your compiled program with `./output`. ## Implementing XOR in Assembly

Let's write a simple assembly program that demonstrates the XOR operation. This program will take two bytes of data, XOR them, and print the result.

XOR Implementation Example

```asm
section .data
```

message db 'Result: ', 0 result db 0

section .text global _start

_start:
; Load two values to XOR mov al, 5   ; First value (5)

mov bl, 3   ; Second value (3)

; Perform XOR operation

128

xor al, bl   ; Result in AL (5 XOR 3)

; Store result mov [result], al

; Output Result

; Use syscall to write to stdout mov rax, 1;   syscall: sys_write

mov rdi, 1   ; file descriptor: stdout mov rsi, message; message to print mov rdx, 8   ; message length syscall

; Output the actual result in a simple way mov rax, 1   ; syscall: sys_write

mov rdi, 1   ; file descriptor: stdout mov rsi, result ; the result byte

mov rdx, 1   ; length (1 byte) syscall

; Exit the program

mov rax, 60   ; syscall: sys_exit xor rdi, rdi   ; status: 0

syscall

` ` `

Explanation

Data Section: This section declares the data the program will use, including the message and the result storage.

Text Section: This contains the actual code (instructions).

XOR Logic:

The values 5 and 3 are loaded into registers AL and BL.

129

Then, the `xor` instruction is used to XOR these values.

The result is stored in the variable `result`.

Output:

The result is printed to the console using system calls. ### Assembling and Running the Code

To run this code, follow the instructions mentioned earlier: create a `.asm` file, assemble it with NASM, link it, and execute it.

Basic XOR Encryption

With the understanding of XOR, we can implement a basic encryption mechanism. The idea is to use a key to XOR with the data we want to encrypt. This method is known as the one-time pad, but in practice, you can use repeating keys for simplicity.

Encryption Example

Here's a simple example that demonstrates XOR encryption:

```asm
asm section .data

plaintext db 'Hello', 0  ; Null-terminated string key db 0xAA  ; XOR key

section .text global _start

_start:

mov rsi, plaintext    ; Pointer to the plaintext

mov rcx, 5    ; Length of the plaintext (5 bytes) mov al, [key]    ; Load XOR key
```

```
encrypt:

xor byte [rsi], al          ; XOR each byte of plaintext
with the key inc rsi  ; Move to the next byte

loop encrypt  ; Repeat for each byte

; Exit the program

mov rax, 60   ; syscall: sys_exit

xor rdi, rdi    ; status: 0 syscall
```
```

### Explanation

**Data Section**: We define the plaintext message and the key for encryption.

**Text Section**: The code reads each byte of the plaintext and applies the XOR operation with the key.

**Looping**: The loop continues until all bytes of the plaintext have been processed.

After running this code, the original message "Hello" will be encrypted in place. You can adapt this by adding another section of code to decrypt the message, which would use the same XOR process since it's symmetric.

While XOR encryption is not secure by modern standards, understanding it forms the foundation for grasping more complex encryption algorithms. Assembly language allows developers to see exactly how data is manipulated at the hardware level, giving insights into the performance and security implications of their implementations.
```

Encrypting and Decrypting Network Traffic Manually

This chapter delves into the intricacies of manual encryption and decryption of network traffic using assembly language. While higher-level languages offer libraries and built-in functions for encryption, understanding the underlying mechanics at a lower level is invaluable for optimizing performance and gaining a deeper appreciation of how cryptographic systems work.

Understand the Basics of Cryptography

Before we dive into assembly programming for encryption, it's important to understand some essential cryptographic concepts:

Symmetric Encryption: This involves the use of a single key for both encryption and decryption. Classic examples include the Advanced Encryption Standard (AES) and the Data Encryption Standard (DES).

Asymmetric Encryption: Involves a pair of keys (public and private). Public keys encrypt the data, while private keys decrypt it. RSA is a notable asymmetric algorithm.

Hash Functions: These convert input data of any size into a fixed-size string of text, which is typically a digest that may uniquely represent the original data (e.g., SHA-256).

For our purposes in assembly, we will focus primarily on symmetric encryption due to its straightforwardness compared to asymmetric cryptography.

Setting Up the Environment

To begin programming in assembly language, you'll need:

An assembler (such as NASM or MASM).

A kernel or operating system that supports low-level programming (Windows, Linux, or MacOS).

A text editor for coding and an understanding of the assembly language syntax for your chosen assembler. ## Basic Encryption Algorithm: XOR

One of the simplest forms of encryption is the XOR cipher, where plaintext is XOR-ed with a key to produce ciphertext and vice versa for decryption. This method is simple yet effective for demonstration purposes.

Assembly Code for XOR Encryption

Below is a small assembly code snippet that demonstrates how to perform encryption and decryption using the XOR method. The example assumes you are using NASM syntax and working on a Linux environment.

```
```assembly section .data
```

key db 0xAA ; simple byte key for XOR encryption plaintext db 'Hello, World!', 0

ciphertext db 13 dup(0) ; space for ciphertext decryptedtext db 13 dup(0) ; space for decryptedtext section .text global _start

_start:

; Encrypting the plaintext lea si, [plaintext]

lea di, [ciphertext]

mov cx, 13 ; Length of the string

133
```

```
encrypt_loop:

lodsb  ; Load byte from plaintext xor al, [key]          ;
XOR with the key

stosb ;  Store  encrypted  byte  in  ciphertext  loop
encrypt_loop

; Decryption is the same as encryption with XOR lea si,
[ciphertext]

lea di, [decryptedtext]

mov cx, 13 ; Length of the string

decrypt_loop:

lodsb  ; Load byte from ciphertext

xor al, [key]  ; XOR with the key to decrypt

stosb ;  Store  decrypted  byte  in  decryptedtext  loop
decrypt_loop

; Exit program (Linux syscall) mov eax, 60          ;
syscall: exit xor edi, edi     ; status 0 syscall
```
```
```

Explanation

Data Section: This is where we define the plaintext, the ciphertext space, and the decryption key.

Text Section: This is where the code lives. The `_start` mark is the entry point of the program.

Encrypt and Decrypt Loops: The loops go through each byte of data, performing the XOR operation with the predefined key.

Exit System Call: Finally, the program exits cleanly.

Compiling and Running

To compile and run the above code on a Linux system:

Save the code in a file named `xor.asm`.

Open a terminal and run the following commands:

```bash
nasm -f elf64 xor.asm -o xor.o ld xor.o -o xor

./xor
```

Understanding the Output

Although the produced ciphertext may not be human-readable, it can be stored or transmitted as it is. Upon executing the program, the data in the `decryptedtext` should match the original plaintext, demonstrating successful encryption and decryption.

Limitations of the XOR Method

While XOR encryption is straightforward and demonstrates the concept, it is not secure for any practical applications due to vulnerability to frequency analysis and pattern recognition. More sophisticated algorithms like AES or ChaCha20 should be utilized in real-world scenarios.

Despite its limitations, the XOR cipher provides a clear example of how encryption can work fundamentally. However, for practical applications, it is crucial to implement more robust algorithms and to utilize library solutions that have been critically reviewed for security.

Chapter 9: Developing a Simple Network Sniffer

A network sniffer allows users to intercept, log, and analyze network traffic for debugging, monitoring, or security auditing purposes. In this chapter, we will demonstrate how to develop a simple network sniffer using assembly language, focusing on the concepts behind packet capture and the interaction with the operating system's network stack.

Overview of Packet Sniffing

Before diving into assembly, let's briefly discuss how packet sniffing works. At a basic level, a network sniffer operates by:

Setting the network interface into promiscuous mode, allowing it to capture all packets on the network segment, regardless of their destination.

Capturing incoming packets and logging relevant header information.

Optionally analyzing the payload for specific data. ### Setting Up the Environment

For our assembly-based sniffer, we'll target a Linux environment due to its widespread support for network programming and assembly language development.

Tools Needed

Assembler: We will use NASM (Netwide Assembler) as it offers a straightforward syntax and good support for Linux system calls.

Binaries: To write and compile our code, you will need

the `gcc` compiler and other basic utilities installed on your Linux system.

Network Access: Ensure the machine you are working on has access to a network interface and sufficient permissions to place it into promiscuous mode.

Understanding the Basics of Assembly Language

Assembly language is a low-level programming language that closely represents a computer's machine code instructions. Each architecture has its instruction set, and in this chapter, we will focus on x86 architecture on Linux.

Key Assembly Concepts

Registers: Small storage locations in your CPU used to speed up operations. Commonly used registers include AX, BX, CX, DX, and the instruction pointer ESP/EIP.

System Calls: Interactions with the operating system, including setting up sockets, reading from files, and managing memory.

Data Representation: Understanding how to represent different data types (e.g., integers, strings) in assembly is crucial.

Step 1: Creating a Raw Socket

We will create a raw socket to capture packets. Raw sockets provide direct access to the network layer. Here's how to set up a raw socket in assembly.

Assembly Code for Creating a Raw Socket

```asm
asm section .data

family_id db 2        ; AF_INET socket_type db 3
    ; SOCK_RAW protocol_type db 0                    ;
IPPROTO_TCP

section .bss socket_descriptor resb 4

section .text global _start

_start:

; sys_socketcall (SYS_SOCKET)

; Setup parameters for socket call xor eax, eax    ; Clear eax

mov al, 102   ; syscall number for socket (SYS_SOCKET)
mov ebx, family_id        ; AF_INET

mov ecx, socket_type      ;   SOCK_RAW    mov    edx,
protocol_type             ; IPPROTO_TCP int 0x80  ;
invoke kernel

; Store socket descriptor mov [socket_descriptor], eax

; Exit syscall xor eax, eax

mov al, 1       ; syscall number for exit

xor ebx, ebx  ; exit code 0 int 0x80
```

Step 2: Setting Promiscuous Mode

To capture all packets, we must place the network interface into promiscuous mode. This step involves manipulating sockets and interface settings.

Assembly Code for Setting Promiscuous Mode

```asm
; Assuming the socket is already created and its descriptor
stored in socket_descriptor

section .data

ifreq db 'eth0', 0    ;    Interface    name    (eth0)
promisc_mode db 1         ; Enable promiscuous mode

section .text global _start

_start:

; ... (Raw socket creation code from the previous step)


; Set the interface to promiscuous mode

; Use the ioctl syscall

mov eax, 16 ; syscall  number  for  ioctl  mov  ebx,
[socket_descriptor] ; socket descriptor mov ecx, ifreq
        ; interface request structure

mov edx, promisc_mode  ; operation (SIOCGIFFLAGS)
int 0x80      ; invoke kernel


; Continue with further implementation...

; Exit syscall xor eax, eax

mov al, 1      ; syscall number for exit

xor ebx, ebx  ; exit code 0 int 0x80
```

Step 3: Capturing Packets

Once the socket is created and configured for promiscuous

mode, we can begin capturing packets. We will read data from the socket in a loop.

Assembly Code for Capturing Packets

```asm
section .bss

buffer resb 4096      ; Allocate buffer for packet capture

section .text global _start

_start:
; ... (Socket creation and promiscuous mode setup)

; Loop to capture packets capture_loop:
; sys_recvfrom (SYS_RECVFROM)

mov eax, 57  ; syscall number for recvfrom mov ebx, [socket_descriptor] ; socket descriptor mov ecx, buffer
               ; buffer for data

mov edx, 4096              ; buffer length xor esi, esi  ; flags

xor edi, edi   ; sender address, null

int 0x80       ; invoke kernel

; Here, you can parse the packet using the data in "buffer"
jmp capture_loop    ; Repeat capturing

; Exit syscall (not reached in normal operation)

xor eax, eax

mov al, 1      ; syscall number for exit

xor ebx, ebx   ; exit code 0 int 0x80
```

```
```

We touched on the foundational aspects of creating a basic network sniffer using assembly language. We covered raw socket creation, setting promiscuous mode, and capturing packets. Although this implementation is simplistic and lacks features such as parsing packet contents or filtering, it serves as a functional introduction to packet sniffing at a low level.

Future implementations could enhance this sniffer with features such as a user interface, packet filtering based on protocols, and logging to files for analysis. Assembly language's low-level nature provides great control but also demands a deeper understanding of system calls and network operations.

Capturing Network Packets in Real-Time with Assembly

This chapter delves into the depths of system programming using Assembly language. By understanding packet capturing at such a low level, we unlock powerful capabilities, foster a deeper understanding of networking protocols, and gain insights into the inner workings of the operating system.

1. Understanding Packet Structures

Before jumping into Assembly programming, it's crucial to understand what a network packet is. A network packet typically consists of two main components: a header and the payload. The header contains metadata such as source and destination IP addresses, protocol types, and checksums, while the payload carries the actual data being

141

transmitted.

The packet structure is governed by various protocols, including Ethernet, IP, TCP, and UDP. Familiarity with these protocols will aid in effectively crafting Assembly code that captures and analyses packets.

1.1 Key Protocols

Ethernet: The most common data link layer protocol that defines the format of packets sent over a network.

IP Protocol: Responsible for routing packets across network boundaries.

TCP/UDP: Transport layer protocols that manage data delivery.

Understanding how these protocols work at a binary level is essential when manipulating packets directly in Assembly language.

2. Setting Up the Environment

To capture network packets using Assembly language, we first need to set up the development environment to allow for direct interaction with network interfaces. Below are the key steps to set up the environment:

2.1 Required Tools

Assembler: An assembler such as NASM (Netwide Assembler) or MASM (Microsoft Macro Assembler) is necessary to compile your code.

Packet Capture Libraries: Libraries such as `libpcap` on Unix-like systems provide an API for capturing packets. While Assembly operates at a lower level, interfacing with such libraries can simplify packet capturing.

2.2 System Permissions

Capturing network packets typically requires elevated privileges. On Unix-like systems, you may need to run your program with `sudo` or set the right capabilities for your binary. Make sure that your user account has the proper permissions to access the packet capture interface.

3. Writing Basic Packet Capture Code

Now that our environment is set up, we can begin writing our first packet-capturing program in Assembly language. This example will focus on using the `libpcap` interface to simplify the process. Here is a high- level outline of the program:

3.1 Code Structure

The code will consist of the following segments:

Initialization of the packet capture process

Capturing packets in a loop

Cleaning up resources

3.2 Sample Assembly Code

Below is a simplified version of how this might look in Assembly language using NASM syntax:

```assembly
section .data
device db "eth0", 0        ; Network device name, null-terminated
errbuf db 256   ; Buffer for error messages
packet db 1518       ; Space to hold a captured packet
section .text global _start
```

```
_start:
; Initialize pcap
; (You'd use syscalls / effects of libpcap here)
; Open the device
; (code to open the device and handle errors would go here)
; Set a packet filter (optional) capture_loop:
; Call pcap_loop to process packets
; (This function will call a user defined callback on each captured packet)
; Process captured packets, display or analyze as needed
jmp capture_loop    ; Keep looping
cleanup:
; Clean up resources
; (code to close the pcap descriptor)
; Exit program
mov eax, 60   ; syscall: exit
xor edi, edi    ; status: 0 syscall
```
```

### 3.3 Explanation of the Code

The above code is highly abstracted and serves as a skeleton to start your packet capturing project. In production code, more details regarding error handling, reading and interpreting network packets, and interoperability with `libpcap` would be necessary. You would often need to create callback functions in Assembly

144
```

that can handle the intercepted packets.

4. Analyzing Captured Packets

After successfully capturing packets, the next step is to analyze them. This involves interpreting the headers and possibly the payload of each packet. Delving deeper, you will manipulate the binary data to extract useful information, such as:

Source and destination IP addresses

Protocol types (TCP/UDP)

Payload size and content

Given the complexity of various data formats, devising parsing routines in Assembly may require significant effort but can be highly rewarding and educative.

5. Optimizing for Performance

Assembly language offers fine-grained control over CPU operations, allowing for optimized performance. When capturing packets, speed and efficiency are paramount. Consider these optimization strategies:

Minimize system calls.

Reduce memory allocation overhead by reusing buffers.

Employ efficient parsing algorithms to quickly interpret packet headers.

By leveraging Assembly for packet capturing, you not only learn about networking at a fundamental level but also deepen your programming prowess.

Parsing and Analyzing Packet Headers Manually

While high-level programming languages simplify this process, there is significant value in understanding how these operations occur at a lower level, particularly in assembly language.

This chapter will delve into the fundamentals of packet header structures, introduce assembly language concepts, and guide you through the process of writing an assembly program to manually parse and analyze packet headers. We'll focus on the Internet Protocol (IP) and Transmission Control Protocol (TCP) headers, discussing their structure and significance in network communications.

Understanding Packet Headers

Before we can parse packet headers, it is essential to understand their structure: ### 1. Internet Protocol (IP) Header

The IP header provides essential information needed to route packets across networks. The format of the IP header (IPv4) is as follows:

Version (4 bits): Indicates the IP version (IPv4 or IPv6).

IHL (4 bits): Internet Header Length; the length of the header in 32-bit words.

Type of Service (8 bits): Specifies the quality of service.

Total Length (16 bits): Total length of the packet (header + data).

Identification (16 bits): Used for fragment reassembly.

Flags (3 bits): Control flags for fragmentation.

Fragment Offset (13 bits): Position of this fragment in the original datagram.

Time to Live (TTL) (8 bits): Limits packet lifetime.

Protocol (8 bits): Indicates the protocol used in the data portion (e.g., TCP, UDP).

Header Checksum (16 bits): Used for error checking.

Source Address (32 bits): IP address of the sender.

Destination Address (32 bits): IP address of the receiver. ### 2. Transmission Control Protocol (TCP) Header

The TCP header establishes a connection between hosts and ensures reliable data transmission. The TCP header format includes:

Source Port (16 bits): Port number of the sender.

Destination Port (16 bits): Port number of the receiver.

Sequence Number (32 bits): Data byte number of the first byte.

Acknowledgment Number (32 bits): Next sequence number expected.

Data Offset (4 bits): Length of the TCP header.

Flags (6 bits): Control flags (URG, ACK, PSH, RST, SYN, FIN).

Window Size (16 bits): Size of the sender's receive window.

Checksum (16 bits): Used for error checking.

Urgent Pointer (16 bits): Pointer to urgent data. ## Assembly Language Overview

Assembly language provides a low-level programming interface that is closely related to machine code. It allows direct manipulation of memory and CPU registers, making it ideal for tasks that require fine control over system resources, such as network packet processing. ### 1. Basic Assembly Concepts

Registers: Small storage locations within the CPU for quick data access.

Instructions: Operations that the CPU can perform, such as addition, subtraction, and memory access.

Memory Addressing: Refers to how data is accessed in memory, including direct and indirect addressing.

2. Tools Required

To write our assembly program for packet header parsing, we'll need:

An assembler (e.g., NASM) to convert assembly code into machine code.

A network interface capable of capturing packets (e.g., libpcap or WinPcap).

A Linux or Windows environment to execute the code. ## Writing the Assembly Program

1. Capturing Packet Data

Before we can parse headers, we must acquire packet data via a packet capture library. The following algorithm depicts the process of capturing packets:

Initialize the packet capture library.

Set the capture filter (IP and TCP packets).

Begin capturing packets in a loop.

For each packet captured, store the raw data. ### 2. Parsing the IP Header

The parsing will begin with the IP header. Below is a simplified assembly code snippet illustrating how to extract the source and destination IP addresses:

```asm
section .data

buffer resb 1500  ; Buffer to hold packet data

section .text global _start

_start:

; Assume 'buffer' is filled with packet data from a capture library

; Offset to the IP header (first 14 bytes for Ethernet header)

mov eax, [buffer + 14 + 12]  ; Load the Source IP Address (offset 14 for Ethernet header + 12) mov ebx, [buffer + 14 + 16]  ; Load the Destination IP Address (offset 14 for Ethernet header + 16)

; Here you'd typically further manipulate the data as needed for analysis.


; Exit program

mov eax, 1    ; syscall: exit xor ebx, ebx    ; status: 0

int 0x80
```

```
```

3. Parsing the TCP Header

Once the IP header is parsed, we can navigate to the TCP header, typically located after the IP header. The following code snippet will show how to extract the source and destination ports:

```asm
asm section .text

; Continuing from above...

; TCP header starts immediately after the IP header

mov eax, [buffer + 14 + 20]  ; Load Source Port (offset 14 + 20 for TCP header) mov ebx, [buffer + 14 + 22] ; Load Destination Port (offset 14 + 22 for TCP header)

; Further processing of TCP data would follow here.

; Exit program

mov eax, 1     ; syscall: exit xor ebx, ebx    ; status: 0

int 0x80
```

Manually parsing and analyzing packet headers in assembly offers a unique glimpse into the inner workings of network communication. While high-level languages provide abstractions and convenience, learning assembly fosters a deeper understanding of how data traverses across networks at the most granular level.

Chapter 10: ICMP and Ping Implementation in Assembly

One of the most recognized applications of ICMP is the Ping utility, which tests the reachability of hosts on an Internet Protocol (IP) network. This chapter delves into the principles of ICMP and provides a detailed implementation of the Ping utility in assembly language.

Understanding ICMP

ICMP operates at the network layer of the Internet Protocol Suite, primarily used for diagnostic and control purposes. It has several message types, including:

Echo Request: Sent by a host to inquire whether another host is reachable.

Echo Reply: Sent back in response to an Echo Request.

Destination Unreachable: Indicates that a destination cannot be reached.

Time Exceeded: Indicates that the time to live (TTL) value of a packet has expired.

In this chapter, we will focus mainly on implementing the Echo Request and Echo Reply messages, which form the basis of the Ping utility.

Setting Up the Environment

Before we can begin coding, we need to set up an assembly language development environment. This includes:

Assembler: Use NASM (Netwide Assembler) or any suitable assembler compatible with your operating system.

Networking Libraries: Access to low-level network libraries or system calls for socket programming. On Linux, we can utilize the BSD sockets API.

Permissions: Ensure you have the necessary permissions to create raw sockets, which are required for sending ICMP packets.

The ICMP Packet Structure

An ICMP packet typically consists of the following fields:

Type: 8 bits, indicating the type of message (e.g., 8 for Echo Request, 0 for Echo Reply).

Code: 8 bits, further defines the message type (usually 0 for Echo messages).

Checksum: 16 bits, for error-checking the ICMP message.

Identifier: 16 bits, identifies the Echo Request/Reply pair.

Sequence Number: 16 bits, used to match requests with replies.

Data: Variable length, contains additional information (optional). ### Example ICMP Packet Format

```plaintext
0  7  8 15 16 23 24 31

+      +

| Type | Code | Checksum|

+      +
```

```
| Identifier   |

+      +

| Sequence Number |

+      +

| Data (variable size) |

+      +
```

Implementing Ping in Assembly

The following assembly code snippet illustrates a simplified Ping implementation using ICMP. This example is for educational purposes and may require further modifications depending on the operating system and hardware.

Assembly Implementation (Linux Example)

```asm
asm section .data

icmp_echorequest db 8        ; Type: 8 for Echo Request icmp_code db 0    ; Code: 0

icmp_id dw 0x1234        ; Identifier icmp_seq dw 1 ; Sequence number icmp_data db 'Ping packet data'
          ; Payload

section .text global _start

_start:

; Create raw socket

mov eax, 102 ; syscall: socket

mov ebx, 2    ; PF_INET
```

```asm
mov ecx, 1    ; SOCK_RAW
int 0x80      ; Linux syscall
mov ebx, eax ; Save socket descriptor
; Prepare ICMP header
lea esi, [icmp_echorequest]


; Calculate checksum (simplified) call checksum
; Send Echo Request
mov eax, 102          ; syscall: sendto push 0     ; No flags
push 16        ; Length of the ICMP packet push icmp_address                    ; Destination IP address
push eax              ; Socket descriptor
mov eax, ds:icmp_buffer            ; Buffer containing ICMP packet int 0x80    ; Send packet
; Wait for Echo Reply
; You would usually implement a receive mechanism here...


; Close socket
mov eax, 6    ; syscall: close
int 0x80      ; Close the socket
; Exit
mov eax, 1    ; syscall: exit
xor ebx, ebx  ; Exit code 0
```

```asm
int 0x80      ; Trigger the syscall
checksum:
; Checksum calculation (simplified)
xor eax, eax   ; Clear EAX
; You would implement checksum calculation logic here...
ret

icmp_address db 0xC0, 0xA8, 0x01, 0x01      ; Example:
192.168.1.1 (replace with target) section .bss
icmp_buffer resb 64; Reserve space for ICMP packet
```
```

### Explanation of the Code

The program begins by creating a raw socket using the `socket()` system call.

The ICMP header is prepared with the appropriate Type, Code, Identifier, and Sequence Number.

A checksum calculation is invoked (implementation omitted for brevity, but it would sum the header fields and data).

The `sendto()` syscall sends the ICMP Echo Request to the target IP address.

The `recvfrom()` syscall would be utilized to wait for an Echo Reply (the implementation of which is not shown here).

Finally, the socket is closed, and the program exits cleanly.

We explored the foundations of ICMP and the Ping utility while implementing a simplified version of it in assembly
```

language. While assembly programming requires a deep understanding of computer architecture and system calls, it provides an invaluable insight into network operations at a low level.

Understanding the ICMP Protocol and Its Role in Networking

The Internet Control Message Protocol (ICMP) is an integral component of the Internet Protocol Suite. It is utilized primarily for sending error messages and operational information that pertain to network conditions. Although it often operates in the background, ICMP plays a crucial role in ensuring that data reaches its destination reliably. This chapter aims to provide an in-depth understanding of ICMP, its functionalities, and its significance in networking.

Overview of ICMP

ICMP is classified as a network layer protocol within the TCP/IP model. It is used by network devices, including routers and hosts, to communicate problems that arise during data transmission. Unlike protocols like TCP and UDP, which facilitate data transfer, ICMP is chiefly concerned with the communication of control messages.

Structure of ICMP Messages

An ICMP message generally consists of the following fields:

Type: This field identifies the type of message being sent. For instance, an Echo Request is represented by Type 8, while an Echo Reply is represented by Type 0.

Code: This field provides further subcategory information regarding the type of the message. For example, an unreachable destination could have several reasons, each indicated by distinct codes.

Checksum: A checksum is included for error-checking within the message to maintain integrity.

Identifier and Sequence Number: These fields are relevant for correlating requests with replies, particularly in echo requests.

Data: The data field may contain additional information related to the message, such as the IP header of the original packet that triggered the ICMP message.

Common ICMP Message Types

Echo Request and Echo Reply (Type 8 and Type 0): These messages are used in the popular `ping` command to test the reachability of a network device.

Destination Unreachable (Type 3): Sent when a router or host cannot forward a packet to its intended destination. It provides information about the reason for the failure (e.g., network unreachability, host unreachability).

Time Exceeded (Type 11): Used when a packet's time to live (TTL) value reaches zero, signaling that the packet has been discarded due to expiring in transit.

Redirect Message (Type 5): Utilized by routers to inform hosts of a more efficient route for reaching a destination.

Role of ICMP in Networking ### Error Handling

One of the primary functions of ICMP is error handling.

157

When a device encounters an issue in packet transmission, it can send an ICMP message back to the sender to inform them of the problem. This feedback mechanism is vital for diagnosing network issues and ensuring efficient data transfer.

Example of Error Handling

Consider a scenario where Host A sends a packet to Host B, but Host B is not reachable. The router, after failing to deliver the packet, can send back an ICMP Destination Unreachable message to Host A, thereby informing it that the intended recipient is not available.

Network Diagnostics

ICMP is indispensable for network diagnostics. Tools like `ping` and `traceroute` utilize ICMP to monitor network health and diagnose connectivity problems.

Ping: The `ping` command sends ICMP Echo Requests to a target host and measures the time it takes for the Echo Replies to return. This is a straightforward way to check if a host is alive and responsive.

Traceroute: The `traceroute` command sends packets with gradually increasing TTL values. As TTL values expire, intermediate routers send back ICMP Time Exceeded messages, allowing the tool to map the route taken by packets to the destination.

Path MTU Discovery

ICMP also plays a role in Path MTU Discovery, which helps determine the optimal packet size for a given network path, thereby reducing fragmentation. When a packet is too large for a segment along its path, an ICMP Fragmentation Needed message is sent back to the source, prompting it to adjust the packet size accordingly.

Security Considerations

While ICMP serves essential functions, it can also introduce vulnerabilities. Certain ICMP messages can be exploited for attacks, such as Denial of Service (DoS) attacks or ICMP flooding. Consequently, many network administrators implement firewalls to control ICMP traffic and mitigate potential risks.

Best Practices

Rate Limiting: Control the rate of ICMP messages to prevent abuse.

Filtering: Configure firewalls to block unauthorized ICMP messages while allowing necessary diagnostic messages.

Logging: Keep logs of ICMP traffic to monitor unusual patterns that may indicate an attack.

ICMP is a pivotal player in the world of networking. Understanding its structure, functionalities, and roles allows network professionals to leverage its capabilities for effective troubleshooting, monitoring, and managing network performance. As networking continues to evolve, the importance of ICMP, while often understated, remains vital in maintaining the operability and efficiency of modern networks.

Writing a Custom Ping Tool Using Assembly

One of the most ubiquitous utilities in this realm is the `ping` command, which is used to check the status of a network connection between two devices. In this chapter, we will explore how to implement a custom ping tool using Assembly language, delving into the lower-level operations that allow for direct control over networking protocols.

By the end of this chapter, you should have a solid understanding of how to craft a simple ping tool that utilizes Internet Control Message Protocol (ICMP), a core part of the Internet Protocol Suite.

Understanding ICMP

Before diving into Assembly, it's crucial to have a solid understanding of what ICMP is and how it operates. ICMP is used for sending control messages across network devices, providing feedback about issues in communication. A `ping` command typically sends an ICMP Echo Request message to a designated host and waits for an ICMP Echo Reply, thus measuring round-trip time and verifying reachability.

ICMP Message Structure

An ICMP Echo Request message consists of:

Type (8 bits): 0x08 for Echo Request

Code (8 bits): 0x00

Checksum (16 bits): Error-checking field

Identifier (16 bits): Unique identifier for the session

Sequence Number (16 bits): Number of the Echo Request

Understanding this structure is vital for constructing our own ping application. ## Setting Up Your Environment

Before writing the code, ensure you have the appropriate tools set up:

Assembler and Linker: You will need an assembler like NASM or FASM and a linker such as `ld`.

Operating System: We will focus on Linux for its robust networking stack and availability of system calls.

Access Rights: Many networking operations require elevated permissions, so ensure you can run your program with the necessary privileges.

Writing the Assembly Code

Here's a step-by-step breakdown of creating our custom ping tool: ### Step 1: Building the ICMP Packet

First, we will construct our ICMP Echo Request packet in Assembly language.

```asm
section .data

icmp_type     db 8    ; ICMP type: Echo Request icmp_code
              db 0         ; Code: 0


icmp_checksum           dw 0         ; Checksum (to be calculated) icmp_identifier     dw 1   ; Identifier

icmp_sequence           dw 1 ;  Sequence   number
icmp_payload        db 'Hello, Ping!', 0
```

Here, we define the structure of the ICMP packet, initializing a message to be sent in the payload. ### Step

2: Calculate Checksum

The checksum is crucial for error-checking the integrity of our ICMP message. We will calculate this using a simple routine.

```asm
asm section .text global _start

_start:

; Code to calculate checksum will go here...

; Use a loop to sum 16-bit words, and apply 1's complement.
```

Step 3: Sending the Packet

To send the ICMP request, we will use raw sockets. Raw sockets enable direct access to the transport layer, allowing us to send custom packets.

```asm
asm
; Create a raw socket
mov eax, 102 ; sys_socketcall
mov ebx, 1    ; SYS_SOCKET
push 0; type (0 = raw)
push 1 ; proto (1 = ICMP)
push 2; domain (AF_INET) mov ecx, esp
int 0x80      ; Call kernel
mov ebx, eax ; Store socket descriptor
```

Step 4: Setting Up Destination Address

We need to prepare the destination IP address. This is typically done using a struct to represent an `sockaddr_in` structure.

```asm
asm section .data

sockaddr_in:

.sin_family  dw 2  ; AF_INET

.sin_port    dw 0  ; Port (not used)

.sin_addr    dd 0xC0A80001 ; Replace with destination IP (192.168.0.1)

; (Ensure to set the correct IP before proceeding to send the packet)
```

Step 5: Sending the Request

Using the socket created earlier, we will now send our ICMP packet.

```asm
asm

; Send packet

mov eax, 102 ; sys_socketcall

mov ebx, 19  ; SYS_SENDTO

push addr sockaddr_in    ; pointer to sockaddr push sizeof sockaddr_in    ; size of sockaddr

push length of icmp_packet  ; length of the ICMP packet
push icmp_packet            ; pointer to the ICMP packet
push ebx       ; socket descriptor
```

```asm
mov ecx, esp
int 0x80        ; Call kernel
```

Step 6: Listening for the Reply

After sending the request, we need to listen for the reply message and handle it appropriately.

```asm
; Code to receive the reply will go here...
```

Compiling and Testing Your Ping Tool

To compile your custom ping tool, use the following commands:

```sh
nasm -f elf32 ping.asm -o ping.o ld -m elf_i386 -o ping ping.o
```

Run your program with elevated privileges to successfully send ICMP Echo Requests:

```sh
sudo ./ping
```

Conclusion

Creating a custom ping tool using Assembly language provides valuable insights into both low-level programming and networking. While Assembly may not be the primary choice for application development today, understanding its operation allows developers to appreciate how operating systems interact with hardware and handle protocols.

We covered the necessary steps to create a barebones ping utility, emphasizing packet construction, checksum calculation, raw socket management, and the handling of network interactions. These foundational skills can serve as building blocks for more advanced networking tools and protocols in the future.

Chapter 11: ARP and MAC Address Manipulation

Understanding these concepts is critical for network programming, system security, and efficient data transmission in computers. We will explore ARP's role in translating IP addresses to MAC addresses, the importance of MAC addresses in network communication, and how to manipulate these addresses using assembly language.

11.1 Overview of ARP and MAC Addresses ### 11.1.1 What is ARP?

ARP stands for Address Resolution Protocol. It operates on the network layer of the OSI model and serves a fundamental purpose: it allows communication at the internet layer by resolving IP addresses into MAC addresses. When a device wants to communicate with another device on a local network, it needs to know the MAC address associated with the target device's IP address.

11.1.2 What is a MAC Address?

A Media Access Control (MAC) address is a unique identifier assigned to a network interface card (NIC) for communications at the data link layer. MAC addresses are typically expressed in a hex format and are essential for the functioning of network technologies like Ethernet. A MAC address is 48 bits long, divided into two parts: the Organizationally Unique Identifier (OUI) and the Network Interface Controller (NIC) specific part.

11.1.3 The Importance of ARP

Without ARP, devices on a local network would not be able to communicate effectively with one another, as they would lack the means to translate IP addresses into physical addresses. ARP requests and replies enable devices to discover one another in a local area network (LAN), contributing significantly to the efficiency of data transfer.

11.2 Reading and Writing ARP Data Structures in Assembly

To manipulate ARP and MAC addresses in assembly language, we first need to understand the data structures used in ARP communication. The ARP message consists of several fields, including:

Hardware Type

Protocol Type

Hardware Address Length

Protocol Address Length

Opcode

Sender Hardware Address

Sender Protocol Address

Target Hardware Address

Target Protocol Address

In assembly, these fields can be read from and written to memory using specific system calls and memory manipulation techniques.

11.2.1 Defining ARP Structure

Here is an example of how you might define the ARP structure in a hypothetical assembly language:

```assembly
section .data

arp_request db 'ARP', 0 ; Protocol

hw_type dw 1                    ;       Hardware       type
(Ethernet) proto_type dw 2048                          ;
Protocol type (IPv4) hw_size db 6;   Hardware   address
length proto_size db 4          ;   Protocol   address
length opcode dw 1  ; Opcode (request)

sender_hw db 0, 0, 0, 0, 0, 0 ; Sender hardware address
(MAC)

sender_proto db 192, 168, 1, 10 ; Sender protocol address
(IP)

target_hw db 0, 0, 0, 0, 0, 0 ; Target hardware address
(MAC)

target_proto db 192, 168, 1, 20 ; Target protocol address
(IP)
```

11.2.2 Sending an ARP Request

To send an ARP request, the assembly code will need to use system calls for network communication. This involves creating a raw socket and sending the constructed ARP packet. Below is a simplified approach:

```assembly
section .text global _start

_start:

; Create a raw socket

mov eax, 41                    ; sys_socket mov ebx, 2
```

; AF_INET mov ecx, 2   ; SOCK_RAW int 0x80 ; syscall

; Fill in ARP request data

; The data preparation process would include copying data

; from the defined ARP structure into a buffer

; Send the ARP request

; This part will involve binding the socket to an interface

; and using the sendto syscall

; Cleanup and close the socket
` ` `

11.3 MAC Address Manipulation ### 11.3.1 Capturing MAC Addresses

To capture MAC addresses, you can listen for ARP requests and responses on the network. This requires configuring the socket for promiscuous mode, allowing it to capture all packets in the network.

` ` `assembly

; Enable promiscuous mode on the interface

; This usually requires using ioctl calls
` ` `

11.3.2 Modifying a MAC Address

Changing a MAC address is often performed for security reasons, or for network testing. The process can generally

169

be achieved using system calls to modify the network interface parameters. Here's a conceptual example:

```assembly
; Change the MAC address of an interface mov eax, 126
    ; sys_ioctl

; Pointer to the modify command structure goes here int 0x80
```

11.4 Security Implications

Understanding ARP and MAC address manipulation opens the door to various security vulnerabilities, such as ARP spoofing. By sending fake ARP messages, an attacker can intercept traffic meant for another device. It is crucial to implement proper security measures, such as enabling dynamic ARP inspection and using VPNs for encrypted communication.

We've explored the feasibility of manipulating ARP and MAC addresses using assembly language. By understanding the low-level interactions with network protocols, developers and security professionals can create more robust applications and protect networked systems against attacks.

Understanding the ARP Protocol and Packet Structure

The Address Resolution Protocol (ARP) is a crucial networking protocol used to map IP addresses to hardware addresses (MAC addresses) in a local area network (LAN). It operates at the link layer of the OSI model, acting as a bridge between the network layer (where IP addresses reside) and the data link layer.

When devices communicate over a network, they must know the MAC address of the destination device to frame the data correctly for transmission. The ARP protocol helps in resolving these addresses dynamically.

In this chapter, we will dive into the structure of ARP packets and how to implement ARP functionality using assembly language. Understanding ARP is vital for networking professionals, embedded systems developers, and anyone interested in low-level network programming.

ARP Packet Structure

ARP packets consist of several fields that provide essential information for resolution. The packet structure is defined as follows:

```
+----------------+----------------+----------------+    +

| Hardware Type  | Protocol Type  |       Hardware Length | Protocol Length |

+----------------+----------------+----------------+    +

| Operation  | Sender Hardware   | Sender Protocol |
Target Hardware  |

+----------------+----------------+----------------+    +

| Target Protocol  | Sender MAC Address| Target MAC Address| Sender IP Address |

+----------------+----------------+----------------+    +
```

171

```
| Target IP Address |

+        +

` ` `
```

Hardware Type (HTYPE): 2 bytes – Indicates the type of hardware used (e.g., Ethernet).

Protocol Type (PTYPE): 2 bytes – Indicates the protocol used at the network layer (e.g., IPv4).

Hardware Length (HLEN): 1 byte – Length of the hardware address (e.g., 6 for Ethernet).

Protocol Length (PLEN): 1 byte – Length of the protocol address (e.g., 4 for IPv4).

Operation (OPER): 2 bytes – Specifies the operation being performed (1 for request, 2 for reply).

Sender Hardware Address (SHA): 6 bytes – Contains the MAC address of the sender.

Sender Protocol Address (SPA): 4 bytes – Contains the IP address of the sender.

Target Hardware Address (THA): 6 bytes – Contains the MAC address of the target (unknown in request).

Target Protocol Address (TPA): 4 bytes – Contains the IP address of the target. ### Example ARP Request Packet

To solidify our understanding, let's look at an example ARP request packet. For our purpose, we will consider an Ethernet environment where we need to find the MAC address corresponding to the IP address 192.168.1.1.

Hardware Type: 0x0001 (Ethernet)

Protocol Type: 0x0800 (IPv4)

Hardware Length: 0x06 (6 bytes for MAC)

Protocol Length: 0x04 (4 bytes for IPv4)

Operation: 0x0001 (ARP request)

Sender MAC Address: 00:1A:2B:3C:4D:5E (example)

- **Sender IP Address**: 192.168.1.2

Target MAC Address: 00:00:00:00:00:00 (unknown in request)

- **Target IP Address**: 192.168.1.1

Implementing ARP in Assembly Language

To implement ARP functionality using assembly language, we will assume a basic understanding of assembly syntax and operations. This example will focus on a pseudo-assembly representation to illustrate the concept without tying itself to a specific assembly dialect.

Pseudocode for Sending ARP Request

```
```assembly section .data

arpRequest db 0x00, 0x01       ;       Hardware    type:
Ethernet db 0x08, 0x00    ; Protocol type: IPv4

db 0x06       ; Hardware length

db 0x04       ; Protocol length

db 0x00, 0x01       ; Operation: ARP request

db 0x00, 0x1A, 0x2B, 0x3C, 0x4D, 0x5E ; Sender MAC db
192, 168, 1, 2 ; Sender IP

db 0x00, 0x00, 0x00, 0x00, 0x00, 0x00 ; Target MAC db
192, 168, 1, 1 ; Target IP
```
```

```
section .text global _start

_start:

; Send ARP request over the network interface

; This part is pseudo-code and would depend on your
environment mov eax, 0x00      ; Initialize socket

; Set up socket options here (address family, type,
protocol) mov ebx, arpRequest    ; Load the address of the
ARP request

; Send ARP request

call sendToNetwork; Custom function to send packet

; We can add error checking and close the socket here

; ...

; Exit the program

mov eax, 1     ; syscall number for exit xor ebx, ebx      ;
return 0

int 0x80
```
``` `

Explanation

In the pseudo-assembly code:

Data Section: We define the ARP request packet in the
`.data` section, using bytes to represent each part of the
packet. The values are filled in according to the structure
we outlined earlier.

Text Section:

We initialize a networking socket (details omitted for
brevity).
```

We load the address of the ARP request into a register and call a hypothetical `sendToNetwork` routine to send the packet out via the network interface.

Finally, we include a standard exit procedure. ## Understanding the Limitations

Working directly with assembly language for ARP can be complex, especially in handling lower-level hardware interactions and specific system calls. The pseudo-assembly example is a simplified abstraction; real implementations would require handling various conditions, error states, and low-level interfacing with the operating system.

We explored the structure of ARP packets and how to implement ARP functionalities using assembly language. While the example here is high-level, the principles translate well into actual implementations on different architectures. Mastering ARP and its packet structure is vital for networking at a low level, whether for building custom network applications or diving deeper into network protocol stacks. Understanding these fundamentals will serve you well as you continue your journey in the world of networking.

Creating and Sending Custom ARP Requests and Responses

ARP operates at the network layer (Layer 3) of the OSI model and translates logical addresses into physical addresses, seamlessly facilitating communication between devices on the same network segment. In this chapter, we will explore how to create and send custom ARP requests and responses using assembly language.

Understanding ARP Packet Structure

Before diving into assembly code, it's important to understand the structure of ARP packets. An ARP frame typically consists of the following fields:

Hardware Type: 2 bytes (indicates the type of hardware, typically Ethernet).

Protocol Type: 2 bytes (indicates the protocol type, typically IPv4).

Hardware Address Length: 1 byte (length of the hardware address).

Protocol Address Length: 1 byte (length of the protocol address).

Operation: 2 bytes (1 for request, 2 for reply).

Sender Hardware Address: 6 bytes (MAC address of the sender).

Sender Protocol Address: 4 bytes (IP address of the sender).

Target Hardware Address: 6 bytes (MAC address of the target).

Target Protocol Address: 4 bytes (IP address of the target). ### Setting Up Environment

Before proceeding, ensure you have a suitable development environment for assembly language. You might need:

An x86 or x64 processor.

An assembler like NASM (Netwide Assembler).

A network interface card (NIC) that allows raw socket manipulation, or a virtual machine to simulate the environment.

Writing an ARP Request in Assembly

To create a custom ARP request, you will fill in the packet structure described previously. We will write a simple example to broadcast an ARP request asking for the MAC address of a device on the network.

Here's a high-level overview of the steps involved:

Initialize a raw socket.

Construct the ARP request packet.

Send the ARP request.

Receive ARP responses.

We'll start with creating the ARP request packet:

```assembly
assembly section .data

arp_request db 0x00, 0x01; Hardware Type (Ethernet)
```

```
db 0x08, 0x00            ; Protocol Type (IPv4) db 0x06
    ; Hardware Address Length

db 0x04      ; Protocol Address Length db 0x00, 0x01
    ; Opcode (Request)

db 0x00, 0x0C, 0x29, 0x78, 0x61, 0xB0 ; Sender MAC db
192, 168, 1, 100     ; Sender IP

db 0x00, 0x00, 0x00, 0x00, 0x00, 0x00 ; Target MAC
(unknown) db 192, 168, 1, 1          ; Target IP
```

177

Building and Sending the Request

Next, we will use system calls to open a raw socket and send the ARP request. Below is an example code structure.

```assembly
```assembly section .text global _start

_start:
; Create a socket
mov eax, 102 ; syscall: socket
mov ebx, 1    ; AF_INET (IPv4)
mov ecx, 2    ; SOCK_RAW
xor edx, edx  ; protocol (0)
int 0x80      ; call kernel
; Store the socket descriptor mov ebx, eax
; Set the destination address
; ... (address setup here)
; Send the ARP request
mov eax, 103 ; syscall: sendto
; Setup sendto arguments here int 0x80  ; call kernel
; Cleanup and exit
mov eax, 1    ; syscall: exit xor ebx, ebx
int 0x80
```

Crafting ARP Responses

Crafting an ARP response follows a similar structure but involves setting the opcode to `0x0002` for reply. The

178
```

main difference lies in filling in the target MAC address with your own and specifying the sender and target IPs appropriately.

```assembly section .data
```

arp_response db 0x00, 0x01   ; Hardware Type (Ethernet) db 0x08, 0x00 ; Protocol Type (IPv4)

```
```

db 0x06   ; Hardware Address Length

db 0x04   ; Protocol Address Length db 0x00, 0x02 ; Opcode (Reply)

db 0x00, 0x0C, 0x29, 0x78, 0x61, 0xB0 ; Sender MAC db 192, 168, 1, 1 ; Sender IP

db 0x00, 0x0C, 0x29, 0x78, 0x61, 0xB1 ; Target MAC db 192, 168, 1, 100   ; Target IP

Sending ARP Responses

To send ARP responses, the process closely mirrors the previously defined request process, involving similar socket operations.

Monitoring ARP Responses

After sending your ARP requests, you may want to monitor the ARP responses. This can be done by setting up a listening socket for incoming ARP packets. By reading from this socket, you can log or process the responses.

While this chapter only scratches the surface—highlighting the basics of ARP and the assembly language needed to manipulate network packets—it serves as a foundational springboard into more advanced topics like packet sniffing, network diagnosis, or even building fully-fledged networking applications.

Conclusion

In this journey through assembly programming for networks and the intricate development of communication protocols, we have explored the foundational concepts, practical applications, and essential techniques that define this critical area of computer science and engineering. By delving into the low-level workings of network communication, we have uncovered the nuances that differentiate high-level programming from the raw power and efficiency of assembly language.

Throughout the chapters, we examined various elements of networking, such as the OSI model, protocol design, and the intricacies of data transmission. We learned the importance of understanding both theoretical principles and practical implementation, discovering how assembly programming can offer unprecedented control over system resources and performance. By constructing our own communication protocols, we have seen how the decisions made at this level can radically impact every aspect of network communication.

The examples and exercises provided throughout this book serve as a stepping stone for readers aspiring to deepen their knowledge and skills in this area. Whether you are an experienced developer seeking to refine your expertise or a newcomer eager to grasp the essentials of network programming, the insights shared here are designed to equip you with the tools necessary for success.

As you move forward, remember that the world of assembly programming and networking is ever-evolving. Continuous learning and adaptation are key to mastering this field. We encourage you to experiment with the concepts presented, contribute to open-source projects, and investigate emerging protocols and technologies. The landscape of networking will only expand, and with it, new opportunities for innovation and creativity.

Thank you for joining us on this enlightening exploration of assembly programming for networks. The skills and knowledge you have gained will not only enhance your programming repertoire but also empower you to tackle the challenges of modern communication systems. As you continue on your journey, we wish you the best in your endeavors and look forward to the remarkable contributions you will make to the field.

Biography

Louis Madson is a passionate innovator and expert in the world of **Madson**, dedicated to sharing knowledge and empowering others through his writing. With a deep understanding of the subject and years of hands-on experience, Louis has become a trusted voice, guiding readers toward mastery with clarity and precision.

Beyond his expertise in **Madson**, Louis is an avid enthusiast of **Assembly programming language**, drawn to its raw power and intricate logic. His fascination with low-level computing fuels his relentless pursuit of knowledge, always pushing the boundaries of what's possible.

When he's not immersed in his craft, Louis enjoys exploring new technologies, solving complex coding puzzles, and inspiring others to embrace the art of problem-solving. His writing is more than just information—it's a **journey of discovery**, designed to ignite curiosity and empower readers to take action.

Through his eBook, Louis Madson invites you to dive deep into **Madson**, equipping you with the tools, insights, and inspiration to turn knowledge into expertise.

Glossary: Assembly Programming for Network

A

Addressing Mode: A method used in assembly language that determines how the operand of an instruction is accessed. Common modes include immediate, direct, indirect, and register addressing.

Assembler: A tool that converts assembly language source code into machine code, making it executable by the hardware.

B

Bitwise Operations: Operations that directly

manipulate bits of binary numbers. Common bitwise operations include AND, OR, NOT, and XOR.

Buffer: A temporary storage area used to hold data while it is being transferred from one place to another, often used in network communication to hold incoming or outgoing packets.

C

CPU (Central Processing Unit): The primary component of a computer that performs most of the processing inside a computer. Understanding how the CPU interacts with memory and network components is vital for efficient assembly programming.

Checksum: A value calculated from a data set to verify its integrity after transmission. In network protocols, checksums help detect errors in data received.

D

Data Packet: A formatted unit of data carried by a packet-switched network. Assembly programming for networks often deals with the manipulation and interpretation of these packets.

Disassembler: A tool that converts machine code back into assembly language, aiding in reverse engineering and debugging.

E

Endianness: The order of bytes in binary representation. In networking, byte order matters as different architectures may interpret the byte sequence differently. The two types of endianness are little-endian and big-endian.

F

Firmware: Low-level software stored in a hardware device, which controls its specific operations. Understanding firmware interactions with hardware can be crucial for assembly programming in network devices.

G

Gateway: A network node that acts as a key stopping point for data on its way to or from other networks. Gateways often perform protocol conversions and are essential in complex network architectures.

H

Hexadecimal: A base-16 number system commonly used in programming and assembly language to represent binary data in a more human-readable form.

I

Interrupt: A signal that temporarily halts the current processor activity, allowing an event (such as receiving a packet) to be processed. Assembly language often utilizes interrupts for event-driven programming.

I/O Operations: Input/Output operations that involve communication between the CPU and external hardware, often using assembly language for low-level manipulation.

J

Jump Instruction: An assembly language instruction that allows the CPU to execute a set of instructions non-sequentially, essential for implementing control flow and loops.

L

Loop: A sequence of instructions that is executed repeatedly until a certain condition is met. Loops are fundamental constructs in assembly programming for processing data streams over networks.

M

Machine Code: A low-level programming language consisting of binary code that a computer's CPU can understand directly.

N

Networking Protocol: A set of rules and conventions for communication between network devices. Knowing the details of specific protocols like TCP/IP is critical for assembly programmers working with networks.

O

Opcode: A portion of a machine language instruction that specifies the operation to be performed. Each opcode corresponds to a particular command in assembly language.

P

Port: An endpoint for communication in an operating system, typically associated with a specific process or service on a device. Network programming often involves using specific ports to establish connections.

Protocol Stack: A set of networking protocols layered in a way that each layer serves the layer above it. Understanding the protocol stack is crucial for effective assembly programming in networking applications.

S

Socket: A software structure that enables communication between processes over a network. Sockets provide a way to send and receive data in various network protocols, especially TCP/IP.

Subroutine: A set of instructions designed to perform a frequently used operation, encapsulating code to promote reuse and modular programming in assembly language.

T

TCP (Transmission Control Protocol): A fundamental protocol for establishing and maintaining a reliable connection between devices over networks. Knowledge of TCP is essential for assembly programmers working on network applications.

Thread: A sequence of executed instructions within a program that can run concurrently with other threads. Understanding multithreading is vital for optimizing network applications.

U

UDP (User Datagram Protocol): A connectionless protocol that allows the transmission of datagrams without the overhead of establishing a connection, often used for streaming applications.

V

Variable: A named storage location in memory that holds data that can change during program execution. Understanding how to manage variable data is crucial in any programming language, including assembly for networking tasks.

W

Wireshark: A popular network protocol analyzer that allows users to capture and examine data packets on a network in real-time, often used for debugging and monitoring in conjunction with assembly programming.

www.ingramcontent.com/pod-product-compliance
Lightning Source LLC
LaVergne TN
LVHW022344060326
832902LV00022B/4238